The Chattahoochee Boys

J SLATER BAKER

THE VILLAGE

I had the good fortune to grow up in a live, work, and play community. The major employer there employed at least one person and often two persons in every residence in the community. Almost everything needed in our daily life was within fifteen to twenty-five minutes walking distance. Within it we had three grocery stores, a drug store, two clothing stores, a U.S. Post Office, three doctors and one dentist office as well as two auto service stations and repair garages.

For our spiritual well being, there were two Baptist churches, one Methodist, one Church of God, and a Church of the Nazarene. For our physical well being there was a sports complex with space for a baseball field, football field and basketball court. To make the community even more exclusive, our homes were built on the edge of a well-designed golf course, the third and fourth greens of which overlooked the beautiful Chattahoochee River. For our educational needs we had only a fifteen minute walk to the elementary school, for grades one through seven, and only a twenty minute walk to public transportation to the high school.

You might ask what was so unusual about growing up in this type community, since mixed-use developments are now being built and promoted as the twenty-first century way of life. But my community was way ahead of its time, for my growing up years were in the 1930's through 1950's.

The employer was a cotton mill and housing was provided at a very reasonable rate to all of the workers and their families. People came in from other areas to seek work in the mill, hoping to improve their lot from eking out their living on small farms, lumber yards and various other jobs. Work was scarce for everyone as the country was coming out of the great depression. My parents had moved to Atlanta when I was six months old. Daddy had worked for several years at a lumber yard when he heard that the cotton mill was looking for loom fixers. He had had previous experience in Tennessee at a silk mill, so he applied for a job and was hired. He would spend the next thirty plus years at the mill. We were given a two-room apartment in a building that was referred to as the "ark" because it was one continuous long building with six units and a barber shop in the end unit, which, by the way, was next door to us.

I was around five years old when we moved to the mill village, and for the first time since my mother and father married we were not living with relatives. Mama told me that she was so glad that we finally had a place of our own that she literally cried when we moved into the small apartment. Even though there would be a lot of hard times ahead, it would also begin a time that she and Daddy would make many friendships that would last for years to come. The village had a feel about it that one would think it was one large family. Folks there would go out of their way to help each other when the need arose. Our family would personally experience this several times over the next thirty years. My parents never hesitated to jump in and help out in any situation. Mama always said she could never repay the kindness extended to us and she lived her life demonstrating that in the way she served others. Daddy, who could fix anything, would often get up early after working all night in the mill and help a neighbor repair his car, washing machine or other appliance. Mama would often help with other ladies in cleaning houses and taking care of children when there was a long illness or death in a family. Many times I saw her go administer a shot to an elderly man because his wife felt she could not do it and also change his bed and soiled clothing, bringing it home to wash and return clean to the household. This was typical of most every neighbor in the village and it was a given that when anyone was in need the people pitched in and helped.

This community spirit was never more evident than when our house burned to the ground, along with five other families' homes. Fortunately, no one was injured. Everyone in the village came to the rescue of all six families by collecting clothes, money, and food, and the mill made room for all of us. We had to share houses until the new construction was completed. One family shared a four-room house with another family. It was "close quarters," with five kids in one side and three kids in the other. Clothes were donated and delivered to a central place and the six families and their children would go and try on clothing and shoes and pick out what they wanted. I know I ended up with more and better clothes than I had before the fire! By that time I had a brother and two sisters, and they made out well, too. Money was collected at all three shifts of the mill, and it was divided equally among the six families.

I still have the list of all the donors and the amount of their donations. This was typical of the heart of the community no matter what the need was, whether fire, death in the family, sickness, someone would step in and organize the effort to help. Many of the families were related to each other, but relative or not it made no difference. Families watched over other children just as their own and in many cases had the authority to discipline the wayward child.

We were poor but never knew it because most of us were in the same social strata. We only became aware of social standing as times would change and so-called progress would come about. We would congregate on neighbor porches to talk about things going on in the city and state of Georgia. We all felt isolated from the things going on in the city until the City of Atlanta annexed our little village and, according to the old-timers, things started going downhill and disrupting their way of life.

Now those of us who were teenagers in those years and are now in our sixties and seventies look back on those days as some of the best days of our lives, when we were carefree and footloose. Perhaps our minds are slipping somewhat and those days may not have been as good as we now remember. A group of us meet together monthly, our numbers gradually dwindling, and the tales are in a lot of cases varied depending on who is telling them! In my case, some stories I was involved in and that are fixed in my memory, are not at all the way they sometimes get told.

The stories that will follow took place primarily in the late thirties, the forties, and fifties. Even my own wife and kids have a hard time believing some of them.

When a famous southern writer was asked how he came up with all his stories, he said, "I just remembered some that never happened." Even though names have been changed so as not to embarrass anyone, someone will surely come along saying they were there and it didn't happen that way. I can only say, let them write their own book!

CHATTAHOOCHEE, GEORGIA

The dedication ceremony at the village store had just ended, during which a plaque was placed on the store steps dedicating them to the gang of boys who used to meet on those same steps when they were young. One of the guys, Robert "Pull" Johnston, had recently died, and his sons wanted to do something to show their appreciation to the rest of us for our lifelong friendship with their father. The plaque simply read "Dedicated to the Chattahoochee Boys." After the speeches and picture taking, the crowd started to thin out except for a few of us who remained to talk about various things that had happened there and the many fond memories of those days of growing up in that area in the late 1930's, the 1940's and 1950's. After everyone had gone I continued to sit there and let the many years roll back in my memory as far as possible.

As I looked directly across the street, I saw the frame building that had been referred to as the "ark." It was a one-story building that had about six two-room apartments in it. At one time, the end apartment had a barber shop. When my family first moved to the village, we lived in the "ark," and we had the two rooms right next door to the barber shop. I was only five years old when we moved there. Daddy had taken a job in the cotton mill. The mill provided homes to the workers for a small charge as one of the benefits of working there; however, if you quit the mill or got fired you had to vacate the home. My memories are a little vague about our life there since I was very young, but I do remember that Mama would not let me play on the front porch because she said she had to keep the front door closed because of all the "cussing" and sometimes fighting that would take place on the barbershop side. On Sundays I could play there. Sometimes Mama would come out on the front porch and watch me as I crossed the street to go over to the post office to get the mail from the Postmistress, who would hand me the mail and tell me who it was from. Obviously, she always read the post cards before giving them to us.

I guess you always remember things that were traumatic, and several things happened that I do remember when I was about six or seven while we lived in the "ark." One such event involved the family that lived in the apartment on the other side of us, who had problems that often led to a lot of screaming and cursing. The husband would come in late on Friday and Saturday nights after an evening of drinking and begin to physically abuse his wife and children. The neighbors would call the police and he would be hauled into jail, but the family would go and bail him out. He would sober up and go to work on Monday and work all week, and then the whole episode would be repeated the next weekend. It all came to a violent head one weekend when he came home on a Friday night and beat his wife very badly and left. He was seen at a local beer joint on Saturday. When he came home that afternoon still drunk, he found that his wife's parents had come and got her and the kids and taken them to the doctor. Upset that she wasn't there, he began to trash the house and left again still in a drunken stupor. On Sunday morning, Mama said I could play on the front porch. When I walked out, I heard someone groaning and crying. I looked over on the porch of our neighbor and saw him lying there totally covered in blood, his clothes ripped to pieces. I ran back in the house and told my parents and they called the police. The police arrived along with a lot of people curious to see what was going on. An ambulance took our neighbor to the hospital, where he survived. After several days, he came home and from that day on was a changed man. Years later I learned that he had been beaten with a bicycle chain, rumored to be administered by the KKK. It seems that our neighbor's wife's father, a bi-vocational Baptist preacher, was a member. But one thing is for sure, the man never beat his wife and kids again. His attackers were never found or probably never looked for. In any event, it was a sobering experience for the neighbor and I don't believe rehab was ever necessary again.

Another event that made a definite impression on me was during a time when the cotton mill had to lay off a lot of workers, my father being one of them. For a period of time he had to take a job on the WPA, a program of the federal government. He would have to leave us on Sunday evening and not return until Friday. The mill allowed those workers to continue to stay in their homes until work would come back to the mill. I did not understand it all then, of course, but later on Daddy told us what those times were like. He would ride with another mill worker who had a car, along with two other men. They would leave late on Sunday evening so they would be on time Monday morning. If they were late or did not show up, there was someone waiting on their job. If you wanted to work you came on time even if you were sick or injured; no excuses were accepted. The pay was one dollar a day. He had to pay a dollar a week to ride to the job in Cedartown, Georgia, and two dollars a week for his room and board, leaving two dollars to give to my mother for her to feed me and my sister and herself and to pay the rent on our place, which was fifty cents a week.

At the time we moved to the mill village, my parents had bought a bed and dresser from a furniture store on Marietta Street in Atlanta on the installment plan. After Daddy's layoff, it was not possible for him to keep up the payments on the furniture. One day while he was out of town working, a truck from the furniture store pulled up in front of our house and two men came to the door and said they were there to pick up the bed and dresser because she was behind on the payments. As they were taking the furniture out, Mama was crying and begging them to wait until another day when my father was there, but they refused. All this time a neighbor had been watching and when my Mama started crying and asking them to wait until Saturday and they would not, the neighbor started crying and screaming at them to the top of her lungs, so that pretty soon other neighbors came out to see what was wrong and they joined in on the verbal abuse of those two men. The men threw the furniture on the truck and took off as fast as they could, with neighbors chasing the truck and still screaming at them. My mother must have been totally humiliated by the whole episode.

I don't remember that night, but I was told that we slept on the mattress on the floor. The next day, a merchant who ran a furniture store in a nearby neighborhood had heard of the incident. That afternoon, he delivered a chest of drawers and a bed to our home. Mama told him we could not pay for it, but he insisted on leaving it anyway. He said he knew my father and that he could pay him for it at any time in the future when he had the money, or, if not, he would consider it a gift to us. Daddy did eventually pay him for it, and after that act of kindness and trust, it goes without saying that anytime thereafter that we needed furniture or floor covering, we would always purchase it from that kind man.. Daddy would never buy anything else on credit after the humiliating experience of having something repossessed. The only exception was when he had the opportunity years later to buy our house from the mill.

MOVING UP

I never ventured very far from the Ark because my mother insisted I stay in her sight. I had heard of a place called the "New Village," and after the mill began to prosper again and Daddy was back at work on a regular basis, he was able to move us to a three-room duplex in the New Village. When we started to move, I found out the New Village was only two streets up from the old village. In my mind, it was a long way from the Ark.

We moved into the duplex that was shared with another mill family, and learned very quickly that they were not too happy to have a family with kids in the house with them. They would bang on the wall if they thought we were being too loud when playing or that our radio was too loud. They had an older son who was in the service and a daughter who was as mean as any boy in the neighborhood. We were told by the daughter to stay on our side of the yard. She drew a line in the front yard and the back yard and even crawled under the floor and drew a line there. She dared you to cross any of the lines. Of course, I took her dare, and she slapped me so hard my ears rang.

As I remember, our relationship with this family never did improve. There was always something to upset them to keep the tension at a high level. The mother was a very nice lady, but father and daughter were cut from the same mold, both downright mean. On one occasion they had bought a new swing glider for their front porch, and one Sunday morning Mama had just polished my younger sister's shoes with black Shinola polish before we went to Sunday School. She was told to go sit on the front porch until the polish on her shoes dried. No one was watching her, so she went over to the neighbor's front porch and crawled up into the new swing, getting black shoe polish on the white swing. The daughter heard someone on their porch and came out and saw all the black polish on the swing and began screaming at my sister, running her off the porch and threatening her that she should never be caught over there again or it would be too bad. Her screams and my sister's crying brought folks out from neighboring houses to see what the commotion was about. Mama, meanwhile, came out with a wet towel and without saying a word to anyone went over to the swing and washed off all of the polish and dried it, took my sister by the hand and went back inside, leaving our neighbor standing there like the crude person she was.

Little things like this kept happening, like my dog getting into their yard and tearing up their morning paper. It even got to the point that we were not allowed to cross their yard to go to the next door neighbor's house. I think it all came to a head the following Christmas, when I had asked for a Long Tom cap pistol set, which featured two Long Tom pistols with dual holsters on one belt. For some reason, I woke up on Christmas morning at two A. M. and saw that Santa Claus had come and there were my pistols hanging on a chair. I eased out of bed and put the belt around my waist and I was ready to face any outlaw. I was standing there in the dark pretending I was having to do a quick draw against an imaginary foe. I did not know that Santa had put in a roll of caps in each gun, and as I drew my guns I pulled the trigger and got off three or four shots before I realized what I was doing. Daddy jumped out of bed, Mama screamed, and I woke up not only my brother and sisters but the "friendly" neighbor. He started banging on the walls and yelling - it was total chaos on both sides of the duplex! After everything calmed down and we were all back in bed, I could hear Daddy trying to muffle his laughter with his pillow. The next morning I had to apologize to the neighbors. About three weeks later, a house became available and they moved two streets away. Their new neighbors had no children. And the new folks who moved into the vacated side of our house were an older couple who liked children!

Living in the New Village had more advantages than the old village, most notably that the toilet was built on the back porch. No longer did we have to walk to the outhouse. The outhouse in the old village was unique in that it was not a dug out pit as most outhouses are, but it was connected to a sewer line that ran directly to the Chattahoochee River. The outhouses were built in quads, with each one serving four families. Each family was assigned their own unit. These toilets were designed with a spring-loaded seat, and when you sat down on it water continually flowed until you got up and the seat would spring back to an upright position, turning the water off. Men did not have to worry about putting the seat back down - that was not an option! Some folks bragged that they had a "country modern outhouse."

The main advantage to me of living in the New Village was the opportunity to meet new friends, making friendships that last even today. One of the first guys I met was Welton "Welt" Stephens. I was sitting on our front porch with my dog Jiggs shortly after we moved in when he came over and introduced himself to me. Welt introduced me to places in the village that I had never been to or even heard about, such as the golf course, the car barns and Grandpa's Ladder. Grandpa's Ladder was a place located on the edge of the golf course where erosion had washed out a huge area around a giant oak tree and the roots were all exposed so that they formed a ladder extending about seven feet that you could climb up or down on. Other places he showed me were the garbage dump, the golf course lake, and the river (which I was never allowed to go to.) I also discovered such things as the Indian cigar tree, rabbit tobacco, the hog pens, cow barns, and the round pond. It was amazing the new world this formerly sheltered boy had found!

Another friend I met was Welt's brother Donnie, probably the world champion marble shooter. No one could beat him. Then there was Carroll "Two Weeks" Evans, who always wanted to borrow a quarter from you and said he would pay you back in two weeks. Unfortunately, or maybe fortunately, I never had a quarter to lend him. Another guy I met, Clarence Chadwick, told me there was no Santa Claus. I told him he was lying but then he convinced me that he knew what I was getting for Christmas because he had seen it. I did not believe him. I had asked for a bicycle and he told me it was in my father's workshop and it was painted red. Sure enough, I was able to look through a crack in the boards and my father had a used bicycle hanging up in there painting it red. He also had bought new tires and a new seat for it. Even though it was a second hand bike, it was like a miracle to me since I had been told they could not afford to get me one. I still believed in Santa Claus. He just only dealt in new bikes and mine was one he had delivered new to someone else three or four Christmases ago.

Another friend I met was Eugene "Bug" Glosson. Bug and I had this ritual with our mothers where we would go to my mother and tell her that Bug's mother had said he could go swimming if she would let me go with him. Naturally, she would say OK, and then we would go to Bug's mother and tell her that my mother said I could go swimming if she would let him go with me. And naturally she would say it was OK with her. This always worked, whether it was swimming, fishing, a movie or almost anything. More than likely they knew what we were doing because they sometimes turned it back on us to get things done. Sometimes when we pulled this trick, Bug's mother would say it would be OK if I helped him finish a chore beforehand, and on occasion my mother would do the same thing. I don't think we ever caught on to the fact that we were the ones being conned.

As I expanded my friendships with these and other guys, the range of areas I was allowed to go to also expanded. I was able to go to places like the river, the golf course, the railroad tracks (even to walking out them to the trestle that crossed the river, a dangerous place to be if you heard a train coming.) Learning experiences came in abundance, such as what areas I could go to and what I should avoid, so as not to get into trouble. I also got to know some of the older guys and marveled at some of the things they did and got away with, or something that was amazing to me, such as the following story.

GIANT SNOWBALL

While we were living in the "Ark," one winter it came a pretty good snow of at least four or five inches. The older generation of guys that occupied the store steps decided they would make the world's largest snowball. They started up at the top of the hill and rolled up a ball about the size of a beach ball to start with. They got some large pieces of burlap cloth that the cotton that was delivered to the mill was covered with. They wrapped the snowball in the burlap and then wet it down, then continued to roll the ball in snow until it became larger, then repeat the process of wrapping it in burlap and wetting it down again. They continued this process over and over. However, when they got about half-way down the hill, the ball was starting to get so big and heavy that it began to be a struggle for them to keep it from getting away from them and taking off down the hill. As they continued to pack snow and burlap on it, two or three of the guys had to stay in front of it to hold it back until finally they got it down to level ground in front of the company store. Continuing to roll it around and pack more snow around it, they finally got it to their liking and the thing was huge, about five feet in height and no telling what the diameter of it was. By the time they had finished, it was getting dark and the store had already closed. There was no traffic to speak of, so they rolled the giant snowball into the middle of the street to leave it for the night. Before they left it, they carried several buckets of water to pour over it.

The next morning, it was frozen solid and could not be moved. Cars went around it with no problem. One of the mill bosses stopped and got out of his car and tried to move it but it wouldn't budge. Some trucks that came through had a little difficulty getting by it, but the drivers took it in stride and laughed about it. After about three days, the mill sent a truck up to get it pushed off the street. The driver was convinced not to destroy it but just to push it up on the sidewalk. It sat there as a monument to those guys for a feat that was never again accomplished, or even attempted as far as I know. With all the snow and burlap wrapped up tight, it finally melted in May of that year.

GRAMMAR SCHOOL YEARS
GRADES 1 - 3

My grammar school years hold a lot of memories for me, both pleasant and unpleasant, but at least I can laugh at the unpleasant ones now. The first grade was a terrifying experience for someone who had been as sheltered as I had been, now being sent out into the world of school with boys and girls from several different areas surrounding the mill village. I'm sure they were just as nervous as I was.

On the first day of school, all the first graders met in the school auditorium. The teachers were seated on the stage. In turn, the teachers stood and called the names of their students, and asked that as your name was called you would stand and then follow your teacher to your assigned classroom. My teacher was Mrs. Doris Curry, a very pretty woman with a little gray mixed in with her dark hair. She was very proper, but friendly, and she made you feel at ease around her. As it turned out, Mrs. Curry would also be my second grade teacher and my third grade teacher. Every time I got promoted, she did, too!

During the second week of first grade, one of those unpleasant experiences took place, but Mrs. Curry was able to keep me from totally embarrassing myself. Just after arriving at school, I realized my stomach was upset and I needed to go to the bathroom, but I was too timid to ask Mrs. Curry for permission. I tried to ignore the urge, hoping it would go away, but that was a big mistake. Finally I got up courage to go to her desk and ask her, and she told me to go ahead but hurry back. But as luck would have it I didn't make it in time to keep from soiling my underwear and pants. So, this little shy first grader was in quite a difficult situation, not wanting to go back to the classroom for fear of being laughed at or teased, but knowing I couldn't stay in the bathroom all day, either. I was in tears, not knowing what to do, when after about twenty minutes Mrs. Curry came looking for me. When she saw my predicament she told me to stop crying and come with her. She took me out the back door of the building so I wouldn't have to walk all the way through the school to the front door. We walked around the building to a side street, then down to the main road where she asked me if I knew the way home. I told her I did. She told me to go on home and she would tell the class I was sick and should be back the next day. Mama let me stay home the next day, and when I did go back, I carried an excuse for being absent, and also a note from her to Mrs. Curry thanking her for what she had done. None of my classmates ever knew what the real story was. I could only imagine what kind of nickname I would have ended up with had they found out. Mrs. Curry never mentioned it to me again, but always after that, in first, second and third grades, anytime I raised my hand to be excused to go to the bathroom, she always granted permission. Mrs. Curry lives on in my heart and mind as my all-time favorite teacher.

Second and third grades were fairly uneventful for me. The only exciting thing I can remember happening at school was the day a couple of third graders were smoking inside the paper house while at recess and accidentally set in on fire. These students were older and really should have been fourth graders. However, they did not pass the third grade, and there was no such thing as social promotion, and summer school was unheard of then. If you failed a grade, you had to repeat the entire year. There were several guys who failed and repeated so many grades that they were able to quit school before they graduated from the seventh grade. The most notable example was James Wilson, who drove his car to school on his sixteenth birthday to tell the principal that he was quitting school that day. Most of the guys who quit ended up working in the cotton mill or the brick yard, or eventually joining the service. I once heard a joke about a guy who refused to be promoted to the seventh grade because he would catch up with his daddy. This could have been a possibility at our school.

FOURTH GRADE

When fourth grade was on the horizon for me, I found out Mrs. Curry would not be going with me, which upset me so much I really wished I didn't have to be promoted! Besides, I had heard that there was one teacher in the fourth grade that everyone dreaded and hoped they would not get. She not only was hard, but was quick to discipline with the ruler or paddle for almost any infraction of her rules. This dreaded one became my teacher! MISS COOPER!

She turned out to be, as rumored, very tough on us and at times unfair. She would give you assignments without giving much time to complete them. She expected, even demanded, good behavior from each of us. There were two boys in the class who were repeating the fourth grade and they delighted in giving her fits! For example, one of them put a pin in her chair cushion and she sat on it. She demanded to know who did it and since no one would confess, she punished the whole class. This blanket punishment happened several times during that year. Since these guys were bigger than the rest of us in the class, we just had to suffer or get beat up for squealing on them. One of her punishments for bad behavior or not doing your work was you had to sit in a chair right beside her desk facing her, which was not as easy as it sounds since she had a bad personal hygiene problem. Enduring that all day was quite a punishment!

Finally the year ended and the fifth grade was ahead.

FIFTH GRADE

Fifth Grade with Mrs. Eberhart as my teacher was very tough. At this age, the boys seemed to be getting territorial, starting to stay with their own group. This sometimes caused dissension when it came to sports, and fights would sometimes break out. Mrs. Eberhart was quick to control the fighting through some stern measures of punishment, so by mid-year it had ceased.

On the other hand, Mrs. Eberhart was always fair. If I did not do well on a test, I could always ask if I could take it over or do extra work to keep up a passing grade. She was also willing to help out with any problems in school or at home. She once did me a big favor, and it happened on Valentine's Day.

Tradition was that on Valentine's Day each class in the school would prepare a large box, decorating it with red and white construction paper and cutting out heart shapes and gluing them on. At the start of the week of Valentine's, the students would start bringing in their Valentine cards and putting them in the box. As the cards were dropped in the box, there was usually a lot of giggling coming from the girls, which made the boys in the class a little nervous, as there were some girls in the class you definitely did NOT want to get a Valentine from, especially the Clinger girls. If you did get an unwanted one, you would never hear the last of it, as fifth grade boys could be relentless in ragging you about it.

Everyone was always excited to see how many Valentines they would get, and, of course, the most popular boy and girl would come out on top. If a boy wanted to give a girl one, he didn't dare sign his name to it, for fear his buddies would find out that he "liked" her. However, if you received one that was unsigned but had a picture of a girl on it saying "Be My Valentine" or some other such phrase, you could later show it to the guys and hint that it was from the prettiest girl in the class. But if, heaven forbid, you got one from a girl and she had signed it, you quickly hid it in your desk (unless, of course, it was from that "prettiest" girl.)

When you got the unsigned cards, even while boasting that you were sure it was from one of the more popular girls, you could get that sinking feeling that it was in fact from the Clinger girl. She was the middle sister of the Clinger sisters, and they all dipped snuff and would spit it out just before entering the school yard. The older sister had once been caught bringing her spit can into class, and was sent to the principal's office where she was told she would be expelled from school if it happened again. These three girls were always trying to talk to the boys and we would try to avoid them as much as possible. Besides, they had a mean older brother who would beat you up if he caught you talking to his sisters. As a matter of fact, the sisters themselves had been known to chase a boy home from school and beat him up!

Valentine's Day came and late in the afternoon, close to time for school to be out, Mrs. Eberhart started to pass out the Valentines. She opened the box, which was full of colorful Valentines, and she would call out the name of who the card was for, but she would not call the name of who it was from. As usual, the most popular kids got several cards. Some of the guys gave each other one of the comic Valentines, which were usually cruel in nature but would bring a laugh from the recipient. As the teacher continued to pass the cards out, most everyone had received a card except me, and I was getting the sickening feeling that I was not going to get one. Could I have been passed over by all my classmates? My seat was right in front of Mrs. Eberhart's desk, and I guess she soon realized that she had not called my name at all. She pulled out the remaining cards onto her desk, and I noticed she was doing something to them before she continued. Then she picked up another card and called the person's name, and without any change in her voice she called my name and handed me a card and immediately called out the next person's name and the next, so that no one could realize that it was the first time my name had been called. I quickly stuck the card in my school book as she finished the rest of the cards.

After I got home and away from all the boys that were walking home together, I opened my book and pulled out the Valentine. It was very evident that Mrs. Eberhart had taken a Valentine and erased the name of who it was intended for and written my name in its place. I was upset about it at first, but soon realized the favor she had done for me, saving me from complete humiliation.

The card was unsigned but it was definitely a girl to boy card and even though it was not for me originally, I tried to imagine it was from the prettiest girl in the class. I was still basking in that thought when suddenly I got a whiff of something that sure smelled like "Bruton Snuff."

SIXTH GRADE

The sixth grade, with Mrs. Annie Sue Peek, was a year of constant turmoil, most likely caused by the students who made up our class. There were several repeaters in the class who were always in trouble. They were guys who were one and two years older than the rest of the class. That year, we were in a portable building that had been set up behind the main school building. Today trailers are used for this purpose, but ours was actually a wooden building hauled in on trucks and put together and roofed. There was no insulation in it so it was constantly cold. In order to stay warm we wore our coats and jackets from about October till April or May.

The school had installed a large potbellied coal heater in the front of the classroom over to the left side of the teacher's desk, so she stayed warm pretty much all the time. A system was worked out in which two boys would be assigned to come to school an hour early to build a fire in the heater. For doing so, they would receive extra credit on their grade. The assignment was alternated so that we all had fire duty every two or three weeks. One cold evening in January, a snow fell and the temperature dropped to around 20 degrees. As luck would have it, Leroy and Eugene, the two boys who were to build the fire the next morning, were both repeaters and among the meanest kids in the class.

When the fire was built each morning, the boys were also to fill a half-gallon can with water and set it on top of the heater to add moisture to the air in the room as it boiled. On this particular morning, with snow on the ground and a 20 degree temperature and all the windows of our classroom closed up tight, the two guys in charge pulled the worst trick of the year. They took the half-gallon can to the cloak room and proceeded to urinate in it, after which they called back other early-arriving boys to participate in the deed! They then took the can and set it on the stove just about the time Mrs. Peek came in to the classroom. Only the guys knew what was about to happen, and they were all watching Mrs. Peek. It wasn't long before the liquid starting boiling and the smell started permeating the room. It took Mrs. Peek only a minute to realize what had taken place, and she quickly ordered all the windows to be raised and the door opened, and made the two culprits carry the can out into the yard and pour out the contents. She told us not to leave the room or close the door until she returned from the principal's office. She flew out the door and marched the two to the principal as we all sat there about to freeze enduring a smell that would not go away. After a while she returned and took us all to the cafeteria to continue our class.

The two ring-leaders were suspended for five days. Others would have been suspended, too, but the two would not name the contributors to the can. The smell still lingered the next morning, even though the windows were left open all night. From then on, the two guys assigned to build the fire were not allowed to place the can of water on the heater until the teacher had inspected it. Then, just to be on the safe side, she made them stick their hand down in the liquid to prove it was fresh water.

Leroy and Eugene became legends who are still remembered sixty-five years later.

SEVENTH GRADE

The seventh grade finally arrived with the teacher Mrs. Collins, who had the reputation of being the toughest teacher in the school,and as far as I was concerned it was true. The best I could manage in her class was barely a C or less. She was constantly on us to study harder and apply ourselves to trying to do better.

One day Mrs. Collins told Earl "Bootsie" Hales and me that if we could make a B on an upcoming test, she would designate us as substitute patrol boys. Somehow we both made it, and were allowed to go to the Fox Theatre and sit in the balcony to see a movie on a Saturday afternoon. The theatre did this for all patrol boys in the Fulton County School System once a month.

Bootsie and I were assigned to be subs for the first graders who lived in the village and brickyard. Little did we know that this was the worst group to control of all. There were two first grade boys who gave the regular patrols fits. One was Richard Smith, who lived in the village, and the other Alfred Brownlee, who lived in the brickyard homes. Bootsie and I were told only that they were trouble and to watch them closely. One week we were called on to substitute for the two regular guys. At the designated time for the first grade to let out, we were to get our group, which the teacher had already lined up for us, to take them home. On this particular day, the teacher had put Richard at the very front of the line, so I agreed to walk at the front of the line. We started out of the school building through the front door, and everything seemed to be going well until we got about fifty yards up the road, at which point there was a trail that veered off through the woods. The trail was used as a shortcut to and from school by the kids who lived in "Larry Town."

Just as we got even with the trail, Richard bolted from the line and ran down the trail. I took off after him since Bootsie had to stay with the other kids. Since Richard was overweight and very slow, I was able to catch him just a short way into the woods. However, he then lay down on the ground and would not get up. There was no way I could lift him to get him back to the road, and when I tried he was fighting me. Since Bootsie couldn't come to help me and I couldn't move him by myself, I didn't know what to do. We were allotted forty-five minutes to get the kids to their release point and get back to school before the rest of the school let out, and I had already spent twenty of that with Richard and we were not very far from school. I finally decided to use a scare tactic. I picked up a large limb that had fallen from a tree and told him that if he did not get up I was going to beat him with it. When I started yelling and hit the ground fairly close to him with the big limb, he jumped up and started crying and ran back to the line. I tossed my weapon away before I was in sight of the other kids, and we continued our trip to the village and let those kids take off to their homes. We had four kids left that we had to get across the railroad tracks safely and then release them. We barely made it back to school before the school day ended.

It was an honor to be a patrol boy. The requirements were pretty tough, including making good grades, but it was a thrill to be able to wear that patrol belt and badge. The free movie was a good incentive, too, and also the chance to qualify for a trip to Washington, D.C. for the safety patrol convention. One of the standards that a patrol boy was judged on was his performance in getting his group of students home on time and keeping them under control with no discipline problems. As the year moved on, the regular patrols that served the village and brickyard students started finding excuses about every other week not to do their job and it would fall to me, Bootsie, and one other substitute to take over for them. The second time Bootsie and I had them, everything was going well. We had Richard under control, and we had not had any trouble with Alfred since the day he saw me bring Richard out of the woods crying and he had told Alfred about the "big stick." But on this particular day, we got to the railroad tracks and just as we were thinking this had been an easy trip, Alfred took off running up the tracks toward the trestle that crossed the river. He was very fast for a first grader. Bootsie and I both took off after him and finally caught up with him when he tripped and fell in the middle of the tracks. He was kicking and fighting us wildly. We had to carry him back, each one of us holding an arm and a leg, and his elbows, knees and face were bleeding from the fall. By the time we got back to the crossing, one of the other kids had run to Alfred's home and got his mother. When she saw what shape he was in, she lit into us with loud verbal abuse, wanting to know what we had done to her son. At that moment, a train came roaring through the crossing, whistle blowing so loud we could not hear what she was saying to us. We all turned around to watch the train, and after the caboose passed by we turned back to Alfred and his mother, but they were not there. Apparently they had left and gone home.

The next time we had duty, Richard bolted into the woods again, and this time Bootsie caught him very easily and brought him back crying. I never asked what happened but Richard behaved the rest of the trip. When we got to the railroad, Alfred took off, but we just let him go as if we did not see him. We released the other kids and started back toward school. After we were a good ways up the road, we looked back and there stood Alfred back at the crossing, so we turned and went on to school. The next time we were called on, Richard took off down the trail, and we let him go and kept walking with the other kids. By the time we got to Bolton Road where we had to stop traffic to get the kids across, Richard had caught up with us and was at the end of the line.

While Richard and Alfred continued to torment the regular patrol boys, we never let them know our secret to getting the group home without incident. Then we found that we could use the two boys as an excuse to delay getting back to school on time, by putting Richard up front to slow down the whole group. Then some days we would put him at the rear to get the group home quicker, and then we'd have more time to stop by the company store and have a Coke or Orange Crush. We got it down to where we could get back to school usually about ten minutes before school let out for the day. School work got harder and my grades slipped and I was taken off the substitute patrol list.

The days went very quickly after Christmas and New Year's. Pretty soon, Spring was on us and I found out that

I was failing so bad that I would have to repeat the seventh grade if I did not bear down and study. My mother would help me on some things by giving out the words for the spelling tests and other memory work. On the weekends, my father would help with the arithmetic work. (Since he worked on the second shift, I hardly saw him during the week, as he was in bed asleep when I left for school and already gone to work when I got home.) Mrs. Collins would let me do extra work or take tests over when I did really bad, especially on history and geography. Finally, crunch time came and it was time to start practicing for the graduation, but after the last test I found out that I only had a 68 average and was going to fail. My parents had already bought my dark pants, white shirt and blue tie, and they were going to be really upset if I did not graduate. My luck had run out on me after six years of just barely getting by - or so I thought.

The teacher of the other seventh grade class was in charge of the music to be sung for the graduation program, and she wanted four boys to sing one verse of "America the Beautiful," but had only three who were willing to do it. Mrs. Collins called me over to where she and the principal were seated, and told me that they had agreed to give me an extra grade if I would be willing to sing in the quartet. I had never sung in anything other than the Vacation Bible School group at church and the thought of doing so was terrifying. But I knew it would be easier to sing than to tell my parents I was not going to graduate. So Mrs. Collins, who always seemed to help me out when I needed it, came through for me again and I was able to "sing for my diploma."

"BOUNCE," THE VILLAGE DOG

One summer day, several of us guys were sitting on the company store steps just passing the time, when he appeared. A big brown and white dog who appeared to be part St. Bernard and part shepherd of some kind. He stood out in the middle of the street just staring at us without any movement at all, as still as a statue. After a few minutes, one of the guys whistled and called to him and he suddenly came to life, wagging his tail and head in excitement, and we called him again and he jumped straight up and came down on all four legs and started to bounce toward us. He did not trot, run or walk; he literally bounced up to us. From then on he was called "Bounce." He came up to the top step and sat down as though he were one of the boys. When you tried to pet him he would jump up on you and begin to lick you in the face. Then he would return to his spot on the top step.

None of us had ever seen him before that day, and when we asked some of the people who came to the store to buy groceries, none of them had ever seen him either.

We soon would learn that "Bounce" had some strange habits. For instance, when he was sitting on the top step and a car went by, he would leap from the top and chase the car, trying to bite the front wheel. He never tried the rear wheel, always the front. After the chase he would return to the steps and bounce right back to the top.

When it came time for all us guys to go home, he would sit there until everyone had left. Then he would leave and go to wherever he was staying. We tried to figure out where this was, and just about every evening one of us would leave and double back to see where he went. But he would go off in a different direction each night. "Bounce" became a familiar sight around the village. He would follow us to the ball field where he would chase balls, gloves, sticks or whatever you would throw for him and he would always return them to our feet. But his favorite thing to chase remained the cars.

One day we were at the lake in the golf course and we discovered that if you showed him a stick and threw it in the lake, he would jump in the lake and retrieve the stick and return it to you to throw again. Another quirky thing he did was when we went down to the Chattahoochee River with a 22 caliber rifle to shoot at passing bottles or cans floating in the river, he made no attempt to go after them. But when you called his name and fired the gun at a spot across the river right at the edge of the water, making a loud pop, he would then jump in the river and swim across to the spot where the mud had flown up and bark several times, then swim back to you. The river at that time had strong undercurrents, and we thought he might get tired and drown, so we decided not to get him to do that trick any more.

After he showed up at the store that day, he literally became the "Village Dog." A lot of people began feeding him and caring for him. One Thursday morning he showed up at our back porch and barked a couple of times. I opened the door and figuring he was hungry I fed him a couple of biscuits and some streak o'lean left over from our breakfast. After he finished his food he left, only to show up at the store steps later that day. After that, he starting showing up at our house every other Thursday at about the same time in the morning for his breakfast. This went on for many months. We later realized after talking with neighbors that he apparently had a schedule of several homes and would show up at them on the appointed day for breakfast at some and dinner at others. We figured he didn't want to slight any of us, and put us all on an every other week rotation.

One food he did like was a Moon Pie and RC Cola, all of the guys' favorite thing to eat. One day not long after he came to the Village, he was watching us eating this favorite snack, and he seemed to be begging for a bite. One of the guys gave him half of his Pie and we filled a pan we got from the store with RC Cola and he really loved it and thereafter expected it every day.

One day "Bounce" was enjoying his favorite sport of chasing cars and biting at the front tire when a freak thing happened. He "caught a car." One of his long fangs got caught either between the tire and the rim or on the hub cap, and he could not get loose and was rolling over and over with each turn of the wheel. The tooth finally broke and he was free. That experience broke him of chasing cars. From then on, whenever a car would come by, he jumped up as though he was going to chase it, but suddenly it seemed he would remember the car he caught and the pain it caused him. He would stare at the car and growl a couple of times and then just lie back down.

Bounce was around the Village for about a year, and all that time we never could find out where he came from or even where he went at night. He never favored any one of us over the other. I think he thought he owned us all. One day, just as he had appeared he disappeared. We never saw him again. He was truly the Village Dog and even today, 50+ years later, when the Chattahoochee Boys get together, somebody always brings a "Bounce" memory to mind.

HALLOWEEN "TRICK NO TREAT"

I guess when I was a kid there was no such thing as "Trick or Treat." I never heard the term until I was grown with kids of my own. Either it had not been invented yet or the folks in the mill village where we lived were too poor to provide any treats. Halloween tricks were just an expected thing, and we village boys put all our imagination to work cooking up some good ones. These tricks were always funny to the pranksters but not to the victims. Two of the more memorable ones come to mind.

The company store was run by Sol Schaffer. When he closed up at night he would place a large board across the back door so that it could not be opened from the outside. The front door opened out. On this particular Halloween, Sol had recently acquired a new meat table and put his old one, a large round table that weighed about two hundred pounds, out back. That night, several guys rolled this table around to the front of the store and somehow managed to get it up about ten steps onto the front of the store. The table was then laid flat and pushed against the front door. The next morning, several of us

45

gathered at the front of the store waiting for Sol to open up at seven-thirty the next morning to see how he was going to get into the store. When he arrived, he naturally did not think it was very funny. He and Abe Cohen attempted to move the table but could not budge it. Forty-five minutes later Sol was begging for help from the guys gathered around, which he got after offering us RC Colas and Moon Pies to put the table back where it came from.

The Mill provided the residents trash and garbage pickup and furnished each family with a fifty-five gallon drum-type garbage can. One Halloween night someone came up with the idea to carry every garbage can, trash and all, over to the company baseball field and set them in the infield and leave them there. (It took the better part of the night to carry out this prank.) The next morning as the sun rose it was a sight to behold to see garbage cans all over the baseball infield and watch as the residents spent most of the day trying to identify their cans to take back to their rightful homes. Since there were no numbers on them, they had to identify their can by the garbage in it! Again a few guys profited from their own prank. They picked up a few quarters by helping carry the cans back to the houses.

Some of the simpler pranks were done not just as Halloween "tricks" but throughout the year. One of them was called "laying out a ditch," and another was "pulling the snake." These were tricks played on drivers unaware of what they were about to meet on the roads of the village.

The first was done by creating the illusion of a ditch going across the road. First, you gather up a large pile of leaves, then, after dark, lay them across the road in a nice straight line across the road. Then you wait for a car to come down the road. When the headlights shined on the neatly laid out leaves, the driver would mistake it for a wide open ditch in the road and hit his brakes to avoid it, sending the car sliding through the leaves until they realized they had been tricked. Some drivers would come out of the car cursing at us, but some would be laughing because they had fallen for the same trick they themselves had participated in years earlier.

Then there was "pull the snake," good for Halloween or any other night. You would get a couple of old stockings from your mother, fill them with paper and tie them together to form a really big snake. Then you'd lay it on the side of the road and tie a string to its head and hide in the bushes on the other side of the road, waiting for a car to come along. As the car approached, you started to slowly pull the snake across the road just as it was picked up in the headlights. The driver would try to run over the snake to kill it, sometimes swerving to make sure he got it. On one occasion, this trick worked the best ever. This driver hit the snake dead center, thinking he had killed the largest snake ever seen in Georgia. Then he stopped his car and backed over it, then ran over it again. He got out of his car to look at it and bent over to make sure it was dead. When he did, the "tricksters" gave one last hard tug on the string and the snake came to life. This guy screamed as though he had been attacked and was scared senseless. But when he heard laughter coming from the bushes, he realized had been tricked. No one stayed around to see if he claimed his trophy nylon snake.

HALLOWEEN "TRICK NO TREAT" CONTINUED

Most of the fun of Halloween revolved around the school carnival which was usually put on by the sixth and seventh grades. Games were set up in different classrooms for a cake walk, throwing darts at balloons, pitching pennies onto a saucer, or the best costume contest. Prizes were awarded whether you won or not. Most prizes were teddy bears, bags of marbles, or candy.

One of the main attractions was the "spook house," usually handled by the seventh grade. The room would be set up with spider webs, skeletons, black bats, and people wearing scary masks. In the middle of the room a table was set up with several bowls on it, one containing spaghetti, one with peeled grapes, others with corn or tomato juice. The lights were turned out and several dim lanterns were set up to cast eerie shadows. A student would lead about ten people at a time through the room to be scared by ghosts and scary characters. When they got to the table, they were asked to feel the brains (spaghetti), eyeballs (peeled grapes), teeth (corn), and blood

49

(tomato juice.) As the girls came by not wanting to feel the "yucky" stuff, Earl and I were under the table which had been covered by a sheet. We had a big piece of ice in a dish pan, and we would hold our hands on the ice and get them really cold, then reach out and grab the girls' legs. They would scream and try to get out of the room, but the students in line waiting to come through thought they were screaming from feeling the contents of the table. They had no idea the girls were having their legs grabbed by an ice cold hand.

After three or four groups came by, we would take about a five minute break while brains, eyeballs, loose teeth and blood were replenished. Earl and I would get out from under the table to stretch and warm our hands. We had stepped out in the hall on one occasion, watching the next groups being lined up to come through the spook house, when Earl noticed that Kathryn, a girl he had a crush on, was in the line. He told me HE wanted to be the one to put cold, icy fingers on HER leg. So we counted the number of students in line and figured out that with two coming to the table at a time, she would stand in front of him. She would be number eight and I would get number seven.

Pretty soon the line came in and we started counting shoes and in a few minutes numbers seven and eight were at the table putting their hands in the bowls. Earl had told me after we got back under the table that he was going to reach all the way up to Kathryn's thigh with his cold hand, and sure enough as we grabbed numbers seven and eight he did what he said - and then we heard blood-curdling screams, the table was knocked backwards, the bowls came off and clattered on the floor, and with a few more loud screams the lights came on as the teachers in charge wanted to see what in the world was going on. As the room calmed down, Earl and I came out from under the table, knowing that what had caused the problem was Earl grabbing Kathryn's thigh. What we did not know was that after we went back in and got under the table, Kathryn's mother had decided to go through the spook house with her daughter. As she got in line with her, she became number eight, while I had Kathryn, number seven.

We were in big trouble. Not only had we caused a near-riot and closed down the spook house, we were now in a room with the door closed with our teacher, the school principal, Kathryn, and her mother. I had to apologize to Kathryn and her mother, but when Earl apologized to Kathryn's mother, he said he thought he was grabbing Kathryn's thigh, which didn't help the situation at all. Our punishment was that we were to clean up the room, get up all the spaghetti, grapes, corn and tomato juice from the floor and mop it. We would have to stay after school the next Monday and Tuesday and clean the blackboards and windows.

We took a lot of kidding from the class. The girls just giggled, but the boys wanted to know how the mother's thigh felt, since she was even more attractive than her daughter. Earl would only grin at them! We were put on probation for two months with threat of suspension from school if we got into any more trouble.

There was another trick that we sometimes played - not necessarily on Halloween, although it would have been a good one, but trouble would have followed had we ever been caught. It had to do with lingerie on clotheslines! Before the days of clothes dryers, women would hang their wash on clotheslines to dry in the sunshine. Usually each household had its own line run beside the house. In one area, two houses were separated by a vacant lot. The clotheslines were very close to the house, leaving plenty of room for games to be played on the lot.

One evening after our games had ended and it was getting close to dark, we noticed that the lines beside each house still had clothes on them, although clothes were usually brought in before dark. On one side of the lot lived a lady who was rather large and on the other side lived a lady who was small and very thin. We noticed both ladies' underwear on the lines, and one of the guys came up with the idea that we swap the underwear on the lines. We hung around until it was dark, and a few of us took down the large underwear while the others took down the small. Then we swapped sides and hurriedly hung the underwear on the opposite lines!

Since we had to go to school, we never got to enjoy the scene the next day, but we understand that there was quite a ruckus around ten in the morning when both ladies came out to take in their laundry. Since we guys were the ones last seen out there, we were suspect. However, our mothers believed us when we said "we would never touch those garments!" Those poor ladies probably dried their lingerie inside after that.

THE BALL GAME

Everyone looked forward to the weekend, because on Saturday the local mill baseball team would play another mill team in the Textile League. The boys especially looked forward to the games with dreams of one day playing on the team, which was to us the Major League. We knew about the real Major Leagues and we all had our favorite teams such as the New York Yankees and the Brooklyn Dodgers as well as the Boston Braves and my personal favorite, the Cincinnati Reds.

We would always be on the ball field long before the game was to be played, mainly to try to be picked as the bat boy or the foul ball chasers. The pay for the job of bat boy would be a broken bat, and for the foul ball chasers a well-used baseball. To get a broken bat that had been used by your favorite player was a big deal. You could take it home and try to force the break back together, put a couple of tacks in it, and then put black tar tape around the handle, usually starting above the break and pulling it real tight and going around and around until you got to the knob of the bat. That bat would be good usually for several of our pick-up games until someone would end up rebreaking it.

The foul ball chasers usually got the much-used ball for us to play with. However, sometimes we "couldn't find" the foul ball, because when one of the better balls went foul down the left field line and into an area where the ground was really soft, the chaser would pretend to be looking for the ball while at the same time be standing on it with one foot, pushing it deep into the soft ground. Then after the game was over and the teams and fans had left, he would be back and retrieve the buried baseball.

The team manager would start to give each of the chasers an old ball, but after giving a few he said that since we had lost two or three new balls that day, the rest of the chasers would just have to go and find those. He would laugh and say he knew there would be no problem finding the "buried treasure." The manager was always generous to us boys, sometimes even giving us a new bat and, when he could, a used glove that one of his players no longer needed.

THE ROUND POND

Located back beyond the ball field and the cow barns, at the edge of the golf course, was a pond that was perfectly round. The "Round Pond" was about ten feet in diameter and about two or three feet deep. Its water source was a spring about 200 yards back into the woods, and no matter what the weather was during the day the water from that spring was always ice cold.

On days during the summer when it was really hot, especially after three or four hours of playing baseball, several of us would go to the Round Pond, leave our clothes on the bank, and relax in the cold refreshing water for a long time. The Pond was off-limits to the girls in the Village because they knew that there would be seven to ten naked boys sitting in it and they had been warned not to come around.

However, many times you could hear giggles coming from the woods and bushes. The giggles would turn into screams and laughter as two or three of the boys would come out of the water, run up on the bank, face in the direction of the giggles and do their best Tarzan yells!

You could never get any girl to admit that she was in the group of gigglers, but if you asked one if she wanted to visit the Round Pond you could tell by the color of her face if she had already been.

THE BALLFIELD

Many of our growing- up days were spent on the ballfield that was located beside the mill and behind the village itself. Most of us could not afford the equipment needed to play any of the sports, so when Fulton County Recreation Department sent a representative to form a recreation program for the kids in the village it was welcomed by all. First they sent an older man whom we simply called "Doc" - I never knew his real name and don't know if anyone else did. The county also furnished all kinds of equipment such as baseballs, bats, and some gloves, as well as basketballs and footballs. "Doc" came two days a week during the fall and winter months and three to four days during the spring and summer months.

Teams were chosen from among the guys who lived in the village and also some from the neighborhoods close by. Usually two guys were selected to choose the teams and a coin was tossed to see who went first. The best players were always picked first, and the rest of us who were either younger or not as good were chosen last. Baseball games would go on until everyone got tired of playing or it got too dark to see the ball. We never worried about what inning it was or who was winning. We just enjoyed playing the game.

One week a new man named Hugo showed up from the County to take over for Doc. No one seemed to know why, but he said he was sent out to take over the program on a temporary basis. He began by telling us he was organizing a baseball team to compete against other recreational teams in the county. He announced that tryouts would begin the next week. There was a lot of excitement over this and we could hardly wait to begin. We would have two teams, one for ages twelve to fifteen and the other for sixteen to eighteen.

The first team to try out was the younger boys, which included me. Hugo would talk to each boy about what position he would like to try out for and schedule his try-out time. When my time came for the interview, he asked me what I thought was my best position and I told him I wanted to try out for "hind catcher" which is what all the boys called it. He broke into laughing and could not stop, and of course everyone standing there did not know why he was laughing so. I sure didn't know what the joke was, until he asked me how many "hinds" I had ever caught! Everyone then started laughing, including the same guys that up until that very minute had called it the same thing.

For the rest of the summer I lived a hard life being known as the "hind catcher." It is a good thing that in that day there was no public address system to announce the starting lineup, as I am sure that my name would have been announced as the starting "hind catcher." Fortunately, when the season ended I was finally able to put the joke "behind me."

SPRING TRAINING/APRIL SHOWERS

As soon as the weather warmed up in the Spring, four of us guys would get a pepper game started to work on our fielding skills. In a pepper game, one guy would bat the ball to us pretty hard, usually on the ground and sometimes a line drive. The games took place in a vacant lot between two of the mill houses. One day by accident we made a discovery that encouraged us to work on our fielding more than ever before. Behind the three guys who were fielding the ball was the house where the family of April, one of the more attractive and endowed teenage girls, lived. Her father had enclosed part of the space under the house and installed a shower. The pine boards he used left some gaps, and on this particular day a ball was hit to me and I missed it. It rolled under April's floor, so I crawled under the house to retrieve it. The ball had rolled up against the shower room and when I reached it I heard someone singing. I looked at the wall and through the gap I saw April in all of her glory, taking a shower and singing. I must have been taking too long to find the ball, for one of the other guys came to help me find it. I motioned him to be quiet and he came over for his turn at the view. Soon all the guys got their turns chasing the baseball under the house.

Spring training time would start every day after we saw April coming down the back steps to go to the shower. One day her brother came out and wanted to participate in our game, so we asked him to do the batting so that the four of us could get more fielding practice. That day we only missed two or three balls because we did not want our inspiration for our dedication to such hard daily practice to become better ball players discovered.

Our secret finally came to light a few weeks later. One of the guys lived in a house directly across the street from our practice area, and his mother would sometimes sit on the porch and watch us practice. She began to notice that our start time and finish time seemed to coincide with the time April would come down the steps to go into her basement with a towel, and also that we seemed to be missing a lot of ground balls and it always took two of us to go under the house to find them. She put two and two together and confronted her son, who 'fessed up. She did not tell on us, knowing it would embarrass April, but we had to change our practice time. It was amazing how much better we became. Suddenly hardly any balls were getting by us and going under the house.

One old gentleman who sat on his back porch and watched us practice commented, "I've never seen a group of guys practice as much as you and still miss so many ground balls, chasing them under that house for days on end. But your practice must have paid off, because overnight all of you started catching everything that was hit to you. Your sudden improvement is a sight to behold."

If he only knew the sight WE beheld!

BASEBALL AND TURNIPS
DON'T MIX

Saturday dawned just like any other beautiful Spring day, with the anticipation of seeing another baseball game between the Whittier Mill team and a team from Fulton Bag Mill. Both teams were in the Textile League and were two of the best in the league. As usual, most of the boys who lived in the village were on the ballfield, which bordered on our back yard, by 8:30 A.M. and we usually did not go home until sundown. The ballgame wouldn't start until later on in the day, so we had plenty of time to play our own game or just horse around for a while.

Around noon we would always get hungry, but we didn't dare go home to get something to eat for fear of being trapped into doing some chore that would prevent us from returning to the ballfield.

At the edge of the field, Mr. Will Joyner usually had a big garden planted and this year was no exception. We always knew that he planted turnips in the Spring and that they should be of eating size by now. So, in order to satisfy our hunger pains, four of us, Welt, Bobby, Lamar and I, decided we would have turnips for lunch. Now Mr. Will Joyner (he was always called Mr. Will Joyner) did not appreciate the fact that he made it possible for us to have lunch without leaving the ballfield, and if he caught you in the act of stealing something from his garden, you had better be fleet of foot.

Just as we were about to have our lunch of the biggest turnips in the field, all of a sudden he was upon us, screaming and charging us like a raging bull. The four of us headed for the creek which separated his garden from the woods on the edge of the golf course, and at that point the decision was made to split into four different directions in order to confuse and possibly lose him. However, as my luck usually ran, he chose to chase *me* and let the others go free.

My best chance of escape would be to head for the golf course and try to outrun him. With Mr. Will Joyner in hot pursuit, I crossed the woods and headed out on a fairway. I knew that about two- thirds of the way up the hill there was a hut that we had built in previous weeks that would offer some safety. I arrived at the hut out of breath from running for my life, and I ducked in and lay very still. In a few minutes he came by mumbling something under his breath and disappeared over the hill at the top of the fairway. Assuming that it was safe to leave, I slowly got out of the hut and started back down the hill.

Suddenly there was a shout and as I turned around I saw him coming over the hill at full speed. Now on this particular hill there grew a weed that we called broom sage. These plants grew close together, and one of the games we boys played was to tie these plants together and then we would run from the top of the hill to the bottom to see who could get down to the bottom without hitting one of the traps and breaking his neck. Mr. Will Joyner was not aware of this game or the traps. As he came over the hill after me at full speed, he unfortunately did not avoid hitting one of the traps, and as he was sailing head over heels in the air I could tell by his scream that I was history if he caught me. After he hit the ground, I chanced a look to see if he was still coming. Sure enough, he must have landed on his feet and never broke stride.

By this time I was not thinking very clearly, and I ran in a direction that would leave me little recourse but to surrender to him. The direction that I took led me to the banks of the Chattahoochee River and to where Proctor Creek comes in to the River. As I approached the creek, I realized that I could not jump it as it was too wide at that point. I considered the River, but the currents were too strong and I probably would have drowned. As I considered my options, I could hear Mr. Will Joyner coming down the river bank yelling that he had me now and to come and take my medicine. He had slowed to a walk by then, and that gave me a little time to look for another escape.

On the bank of the creek was an old dead tree that had a hollow place deep down under the bottom that was big enough for me to get into. However, there was a potential problem with that. I did not know what may be in that tree at this time! Suddenly I heard Mr. Will Joyner yell even louder, and I knew that whatever was in that hole could not possibly be as mean as he was, so into the hole I went. Not daring to move a muscle or even breathe, I lay still as he walked around the tree and up and down the creek bank, talking to himself about where I could be. After what seemed like an eternity, he finally left.

I stayed in the tree at least another thirty minutes before ever daring to look out. I took another route home, following the creek bank which would lead me at least two miles out of the way, but I felt it would be the safest route to take. When I finally got home, I figured I needed to change clothes before going back to the ballfield, so that maybe Mr. Will Joyner would not recognize me. I finally got up enough courage to return to the field to see what there was left of the game. Upon arriving at the field I noticed that the other three guys had also gone home and changed clothes! And the game was in the ninth inning - I had missed the whole thing.

Oh, yes, one other thing I noticed was Mr. Will Joyner seated on the bottom row of the left field bleachers eating a TURNIP!

THE GAMBLERS

On game days, the small right field bleacher area which only held about fifty fans was occupied by the betting crowd, most of whom were feeling no pain by the time the game started. They had started their drinking for the day at home with beer, and continued with whatever else was on hand at the ballfield wrapped in a brown paper bag. The gamblers would bet on what the next batter would do at his time at bat, whether he would fly out or strike out or get a hit.

The odds were usually even. A bet of one dollar would be made by one of the men on a fly ball, two or three or more would say "I'll cover that" and so it would go the whole game. In the process of all this money being passed up and down the rows of the bleachers, sometimes a dollar bill would miss the hand reaching for it and it would fall under the stands and none of them would make any attempt to retrieve it.

We boys soon learned that it could be profitable to crawl up under the stands and wait for the money to fall. The hazard was that you had to endure the dropped cigarettes and cigars hitting you, or the spilled beer and, of course, spit bouncing off your head. The guy who won the bet probably never got the full amount of his winnings, but never seemed to care because he was so out of it. There was never much competition from other boys to work the stands because of the conditions under there. The three of us who dared usually, instead of trying to grab the money that fell, just spread out under there and gathered it up and divided it up three ways later. That way, we didn't have to dodge the cigarettes, cigars, beer and spit.

Gambling was illegal, but on a hot Saturday afternoon it was apparently overlooked. Could be because most of the time an off-duty law officer was in the stands. I don't remember there ever being more than three or four dollar bills and maybe a few quarters falling through on any given day, but that was more than most of us boys would see in a month. Some days nothing would fall through except an unlit cigarette or cigar, which you could sell to a friend for two cents, or up to a nickel for the cigar. One game an unopened pack of Chesterfields fell through, which in turn was bartered for a coke each for the three of us.

After the game was over and most of the fans had left and the ball players had gone to the clubhouse for showers, those gamblers would still be sitting out there on the bleachers, betting on fly balls!

KILLING RATS

You can tell you're hard up for something to do when one of your favorite pastimes is killing rats.

In the area behind the baseball field was a section that was set aside for the families who wanted to to raise hogs and keep cows. The hog pens attracted rats, and when I say rats I mean large wharf rats, some the size of a cat or small dog.

The rats lived underground in a series of holes and tunnels that ran for great lengths through the hog pen area. The tunnels would connect and travel in every direction. There were two ways that could be used to get the rats out of those holes in order to kill them, the water method and the gasoline method.

The water method involved hooking a hose to a nearby water faucet and inserting it into a hole. However, it couldn't be just any hole. You had to find a hole that looked like it went straight down into the ground three or four feet and then turn the water on full blast. Each guy would then station himself at one of the many holes armed with a stick or a ball bat. Usually the weapon of choice was a "picker stick," used in the cotton mill on the looms. The stick itself was made out of a very hard wood of some sort and it was small on one end and larger and weighted on the other end. When the stick was used on a loom, its purpose was to catch a steel headed shuttle that was being thrown across the loom at about eighty miles per hour. The shuttle contained a spool of thread used to weave the cloth being produced in the mill.

After you had stationed yourself at your hole, you would stand there waiting for the water to show up. If you were lucky, the water would soon show up in your hole and you would know you picked the right tunnel. As you stood there anticipating the rat to come out of your hole, you knew you would probably get only one good shot at him when he came out. You could tell when he was about ready to come out. The water would rise up about level with the top of the hole and stand that way for two or three minutes and then the water would suddenly drop and the rat would come out at top speed. If you were not ready, you could find yourself with a large rat climbing up your leg. You were usually as shocked as the rat was when he came out of the hole, but if you missed him there were always a couple of dogs around that would chase the rat down.

And then there was the gasoline method. You would take a large spray gun and fill it with gasoline and spray the fine mist of gas into the hole for several minutes, then step back and throw a lighted match into the hole. An explosion would occur and fire would come out every hole connected to that tunnel. It was advisable to stand clear of the hole until after the explosion! Shortly, any rats that were in there came out with their fur on fire. Due to the smell that method caused, the water method was preferred.

We did our part to hold down the rat population in the village. But I wonder what the animal rights activists would say today about our methods?

SOMEONE'S WATCHING

Times were hard and money was scarce for the people who worked in the cotton mill and lived in the village. In most families, both husband and wife worked and many times they worked on different shifts. This in turn left a lot of kids without parental supervision. Third shift workers usually came home and went to bed for a few hours, while the other parent worked on the first shift. This situation of lack of parental supervision was somewhat offset by the fact that families in the village looked out for each other's children. In other words, you had more than one Mama or Daddy all over the village watching you just as they would their own child. In some cases there was an understanding that any parent in the village had the authority to discipline the wayward child. And a report to your parents on the problem you were causing usually meant more severe punishment than if your own parents caught you in the act. There was one time that I was a prime example of the consequences of this network of watchful parents.

Mama and Daddy were going to visit relatives and would be gone all day. I was left in charge of my younger brother who was about eight years old. I was told very clearly not to go to Nickajack Creek swimming. But not long after they left, along came four of my buddies on their way to the Creek, trying their best to entice me to go along with them. I explained to them that I was told not to go and that I had to watch my brother, but they continued to plead with me to come and bring my brother along and they would help watch him, and, besides, we would be back home long before my parents were to return. This made sense to me, since they would never know that I had disobeyed them if I was back before they returned. I went along, never dreaming what lay ahead of me because of the willful breaking of the one and only rule that I was given.

When we arrived at the creek, I sat my brother down on the bank of the Creek and told him not to move or even get close to the water, because he could not swim at all. I checked on him every few minutes and he would still be where I put him, playing in the sand. I don't know how much time went by as we were engrossed in a game of tag in the creek, when I suddenly realized my brother was no longer on the bank. I yelled for him but got no answer. I got out of the creek and started searching for him, all the while calling him at the top of my voice, and my friends were doing the same thing in the other direction.

About thirty yards down the creek a sand pump was in operation, pumping sand from the middle of the creek. When these sand pumps were working, they pumped large amounts of sand out, which was sold to construction firms. We would often move our swimming hole to the last pumping operation because it would mean the water would be about ten feet in depth. As I walked closer to the pumping operation, I heard the men working the pump suddenly start yelling, and one of the men jumped into the creek and went under the water.

When he came up, he had my brother with him, coughing, crying, and spitting up water. The man brought him to the creek bank, and I grabbed him and pulled him out of the water. Apparently, my brother had heard the sand pump working and wandered off to see what was going on. The men did not see him at first, only when he walked up to the edge of the bank and slipped and fell into the deepest part of the creek. The pump operator immediately jumped in, pulling him to safety.

All the way home I kept talking to my brother, telling him he was not to say anything about the fact that we had gone to the creek, and definitely not mention a word about his falling in and having to be saved. I put the fear into him that he and I both would get the worst whipping that we had ever gotten.

When our parents returned that evening they asked if we had any problems while they were away and I assured them that there were none. My brother did as he was told and kept his mouth shut, and I thought I was in the clear. However, on Monday when my Daddy returned to work, a man who worked in the mill on the same shift came up to him and asked how his young son was doing, and, of course, Daddy having no idea what the man was talking about said he was doing fine and why was he asking. The man proceeded to tell him about the incident at the creek on Saturday and how he had to dive into about ten feet of water and pull my brother out. Of all the men who worked in the mill, that this one had to be working on the same shift with my father proved to me that day that you cannot disobey your parents and get away with it.

Daddy worked on the second shift, three-thirty to eleven-thirty at night. The next morning he came in the room where I was sleeping and woke me up around eight a.m. and told me to come to the kitchen and closed the door. I knew immediately that I was in deep trouble and that he had heard about the incident at the creek. He asked me why I disobeyed him and pointed out to me that my doing so almost cost my brother his life. At the same time he was removing his leather belt, and without saying another word he began giving me the worst whipping I ever had, leaving stripes on my back and legs. It continued until Mama finally got between us and stopped him. This was one of only two whippings I ever remember getting from him, since he usually left the discipline up to my mother. Although it was severe, I never blamed him. My parents had already lost one child, and the thoughts of what could have happened probably increased the severity of my punishment.

So growing up with so many extra pairs of eyes watching us really encouraged us to behave ourselves, especially when adults were around. If another parent reported something to your parents, there was no appeal. You were guilty.

THE SWIMMING HOLE

Our swimming hole was located in Proctor Creek, which ran from somewhere in Atlanta into the Chattahoochee River. At a point in the creek off Parrott Avenue in the village, sand had been pumped from the creek by a local sand and gravel business. This pumping of sand left a hole in the middle of the creek about eight feet deep. This deep hole made a perfect spot for diving out of trees or from the cable that someone years ago had stretched across the creek.

The swimming hole was located about seventy-five yards off the road and was secluded from passing cars. Since no one could see us, we were able to swim in the nude. Occasionally someone would walk upon us but they would usually turn around and go the other way. However, on one occasion when there were about a dozen guys in the water having a good time just tossing a ball or playing tag, all of a sudden we heard laughing and screaming coming from the bushes that lined the creek bank about twenty yards from the water. We started yelling "Who's up there?" At that point ten Negro teenage girls stood up in the bushes. The girls were from an area called the

Brickyard, where Chattahoochee Brick Company was located. We started telling them to go away and leave us alone, but all they would do is laugh.

Not only was their laughing annoying us, but we had a slight problem regarding our clothes, which were on the bank between them and the creek. We were not going to be able to get to our clothes without the girls getting an eyeful.

They all continued to laugh and argue with us that they were not going to leave. After about ten minutes of this, they all came out of the bushes and sat down on our clothes and continued their taunting of us to come and get our clothes. No one was brave enough to volunteer to run out of the water to see what they would do, so we decided that on the count of three, we would all run toward the girls with a rebel yell to scare them away. We warned them this was going to happen; however, they chose not to believe us and dared us to come on. So at the count of three, twelve naked white boys came charging out of Proctor Creek screaming to the tops of our lungs, at which time the Negro girls all stood up off our clothes and started pointing their fingers at our private parts, making rather disparaging remarks while laughing hysterically!

They finally ran to the road and we scrambled to put on our clothes. Totally embarrassed by this encounter, we vowed not to mention it to anyone except among ourselves. And the kidding went on for months as to which one of us the Negro girls found to be the most amusing sight!

We continued to have many happy days in our swimming hole until the gas and oil company bought Moore's Pasture and cleared all of the trees and graded the hills to build huge storage tanks in the entire area. They also cleared the other side of the road, laying bare the creek. They built an office building right on the road overlooking the creek. We continued to swim there until one day as we swam (in the nude as always) a man from the oil company walked up and told us that we could no longer swim there because the women in his office could see us! We felt that he did not have the authority to stop us, so we made remarks like "tell them to quit looking" and "tell them to come and join us on their lunch hour." He didn't think it was funny and told us we would have to move farther downstream or put on a bathing suit. One of our intellectuals asked him what was a "bathing suit?" None of us owned one, and besides, we were not bathing. We did that in a #2 washtub on Saturday nights!

The oil company man left very angry. The next day we were back and this time he showed up with two other men who informed us that they owned the property and insisted that we get our clothes and leave immediately or they would call the police and have us arrested for trespassing and indecency. We got out of the water, put our clothes on and walked by the building, waving goodbye to the women who were standing at the windows watching us leave.

We later found another nice swimming hole on Nickajack Creek. The only problem we had with it was we never could pronounce it correctly.

CHRISTMAS BOOTS

The rule in our family at Christmas was that we could only choose one thing that we wanted to find under the tree, and this year all I wanted was a pair of boots. Most of the guys I ran with already had hunting boots and I was always envious of them. I was determined to pick out a pair that would show up any other pair of boots around.

My daddy took me to Sears & Roebuck out on Ponce de Leon Avenue to pick out the pair I would like. I tried on three or four pairs, but they were nothing special and I asked to go to another store. As we were about to leave, I spotted a pair up on a display rack that was not in the regular area of where the other boots were displayed. This pair was what I had been looking for! They were genuine leather, light tan with rawhide strings. But the best feature was that on the right boot on the outside was a pocket knife holder with a snap cover on it, and inside the pocket was a genuine pearl handled Barlow knife. I knew I would be the envy of all the guys with this pair of hunting boots.

After we got a pair for me to try on, Daddy asked the clerk what the price was. He told us they were $9.95 because of the knife pocket and that the knife was extra. Daddy said we could not afford that, and that I would have to settle for a plain pair like the ones I had tried on which cost $6.50. We left the store with no boots, since Daddy said that we could look somewhere else to see if we could find something similar to the pair I wanted. Later on, he told me he could not find anything like what I wanted and that if I wanted boots I would have to take the plain ones. I told him that was all right, but I would at least like to have the rawhide strings in them rather than the standard strings. I was really disappointed, but accepted the fact that I would have ordinary boots like the other guys.

It was only about a week till Christmas, so I had to put the fancy boots out of my mind and just wait to see what I got. Christmas morning finally arrived and when I went to the Christmas tree I could not find any boots of any kind. (Our Christmas presents were never wrapped, but just sat under the tree.) I was getting upset when I looked over against the wall and there sat the pair of boots that I wanted. I could not believe that I had gotten them after I was told we could not afford them! The only difference was that the knife pocket did not contain the genuine pearl-handle Barlow knife, but there was a three-blade bone handle Case knife instead. It seems that Daddy was able to get the boots cheaper without the Barlow knife. I could tell that the Case knife was not brand new, but I didn't mind because any boy would rather have a three-blade bone handle Case than a two-blade pearl handle Barlow. Daddy had bought the Case knife from a friend (for probably next to nothing), and sharpened all three blades to a razor-like edge. I finally had something that no other boy in the Village had at that time, and all of them were envious of the boots with that secret knife holder. I made sure they were cleaned and shined every day. Little did I know that the pride I had in my boots was about to vanish.

One morning at 3 A.M. around the second week in January, we were awakened by the family in the other side of our duplex pounding on the walls and someone else pounding on our front door. They were screaming "Fire, fire, get out quick." I remember my mama screaming at us to get up and get out of the house. My younger brother and I slept in the front room next to a window and someone was banging on the window. We jumped up and ran out on the front porch. I realized then that I had no pants on and ran back and grabbed them off the bed post and ran back out. The temperature was in the low teens and we were all bare-footed. Mama made sure we were all accounted for and led us up the street to a neighbor's house. By the time we got there we were all so cold we could not even feel our feet. The neighbors gave us a blanket to wrap up in and got a fire started in a heater.

We lost everything we had except for one chest of drawers that held only bed linens and blankets. I found out later that the only reason we got that is that my daddy, who since the Depression had not trusted banks, had all his savings in silver dollars in a metal foot locker in the closet of the middle room. He had run back into the house to try to get the trunk, but the smoke was too thick. As he was coming back out he ran into the chest of drawers which was near the front door, so he pushed it out onto the porch and two men picked it up and carried it away from the fire. Before the fire was out it had totally destroyed three duplexes and left six families homeless. Fortunately, four of the families had relatives living in the village and were able to move in with them. There was one four- room house that was vacant, and we were given two rooms and the other family two rooms until something more permanent could be worked out.

After we were taken to the neighbor's house, it dawned on me that my boots and case knife were now ashes. I had worn them and showed them off for only about three weeks! I started in on my parents that I had to have some new boots just like the ones that burned in the fire, but they let me know right away that we had no money to buy clothes and shoes, much less new boots. The community got together and started collecting used clothes and shoes from other families who had some to share. The people who gathered up the items would bring them by the houses where the burned-out families were staying and we would go through them and try on anything that looked like it might fit. My brother and I were able to find some overalls and shirts that fit us, but trying on used shoes was not so easy. However, after going through several boxes of shoes I came across a pair of old boots that fit but needed new soles and heels badly, but I took them. Daddy put new soles and heels on them and they worked out fine. I have no idea who the boots belonged to, nor did they compare to my Christmas boots, but I was glad and thankful to have them. I kept them cleaned and shined until I outgrew them, but I never forgot my light tan hunting boots with the secret knife holder and the bone handle Case knife.

THE CHRISTMAS GIFT

When I was twelve years old, girls were the farthest thing from my mind. However, there was a girl who lived in the house two doors down who apparently "liked" me without my knowing it. The day before Christmas Eve she brought me a present all wrapped up in red paper with a nice bow on it. I was not home when she brought it by and she left it with my sisters, who were dying for me to come home so that the teasing could begin. They were sitting in the kitchen with my mother and brother when I came in, and they starting gleefully chanting "you've got a girlfriend, you've got a girlfriend." I was yelling at them and threatening them, still not knowing what they were talking about. Finally, they gave me the neatly wrapped package, urging me to open it in front of them, which I refused to do. They started begging Daddy to make me open it, and when he told me I had to, I reluctantly proceeded to tear off the red paper, not knowing what to expect.

The gift turned out to be a genuine leather billfold. Upon opening it up, I could tell there was a picture in it, and of course my sisters started in on me that the girl had put her picture in it for me to look at. Much to my relief, it was not of her but of Greer Garson, the movie star.

My mother then told me that I was going to have to get her a present, since she had given me one. I protested and I think I even cried and told her there was no way I was going to do that. But she insisted, and I was totally humiliated and could only imagine what my buddies would do and the flak I would get from them.

The next morning my parents had to make a trip to the grocery store and they assured me they would find a nice gift for me to give to the girl that day, which was Christmas Eve. I threatened to run away, or at least stay away somewhere until after Christmas! When they returned from the store, Mama had bought two glass candle holders that each held two candles, and she included four red candles to go with them. She wrapped them in white tissue paper and tied the package up with ribbon, handed it to me and told me I had to take it to the girl's house and give it to her personally. I couldn't believe it! I was mortified.

I left with the package, but as soon as I was out of her sight I circled back and went into our outhouse, stayed in there long enough to have had time to deliver the present, and left it in the outhouse, planning to go back and get it and dispose of it later. My plan backfired when my younger brother came into the house carrying the present and telling where he had found it!

And so, under the watchful eye of my father and his belt, I was sent to deliver the present. He walked with me far enough to see me go up to the door, where I was to knock and hand it to her. Mad, scared, humiliated and in shock at what I was being made to do, I finally knocked on the door. No one answered.

I looked over at Daddy and he told me to knock harder. I picked up a rock then, determined to get this over with. I banged the rock on the door as hard as I could. Luck was on my side, and no one was home, so I set the package behind the screen door and left, Daddy being my witness that I had made a valiant effort.

I guess the girl shared my opinion that glass candle holders and four red candles was a dumb gift for an eleven-year-old girl. She never spoke to me again until I was sixteen, and in all that time no mention of my gift to her was ever made. The red candles *were* kind of pretty, though.

MOORE'S PASTURE

Moore's Pasture was one of my favorite places to play when I was a child. It was just down the street from where we lived. Even though it was called a pasture, it had a large area that was wooded. This is the place where we played most of our games, especially a game we called "Kack." It was really a follow-the-leader game, and I never knew why it was called "Kack." This is also the place I would like to go to be by myself when I felt the need for solitude.

One day late in the afternoon I was sitting on a tree limb about ten feet off the ground when I heard a noise like someone coming through the woods. I pulled myself up and got behind the trunk of the tree to hide from whoever it was coming by. I sat there waiting to see who it was when suddenly the sound stopped, as though the person was trying to listen to see whether they were alone. I still could not see anyone or anything. Sometimes a cow would venture from the pasture down into the woods. There was also a large bull that was kept in the field along with the cows. Not knowing what to expect,

I waited in the tree for what seemed like an eternity, but still nothing moved.

After I'd waited as long as I could, I decided to climb down out of the tree. Back on the ground, I moved very quietly toward the direction I first heard the sound. I heard something behind me and turned around quickly to find nothing there, then heard movement to my left and the sound of twigs cracking and bushes moving. Starting to wonder if I should have come down from my safe perch, I stopped behind another large tree to watch and listen, but nothing was moving anywhere, only the sound of birds singing and an occasional car going up the road. By the time the sun was starting to set, I was feeling spooked and started moving slowly toward the road. It was then that I caught a glimpse of something moving through the tall bushes to my right and there it stopped. Circling around the other side of the bushes, I saw movement of something white like clothing so I knew then it was human and not that big animal I had feared. I moved a little closer and saw from the back that it was a girl crouching down in the tall grass.

I could not tell who she was, but I decided I would give her the scare of her life. I ran up and grabbed her from behind. She screamed loud enough for everyone in the village to hear and almost fainted. She was crying hysterically and as I was trying to get her to calm down she turned around and I was shocked to see that it was the girl who years earlier had given me the Christmas gift, a billfold. I apologized for scaring the daylights out of her but said I'd thought it was someone playing a trick on me. She finally quit crying and I asked her why she was in the pasture to begin with. She said she had seen me go by her house and followed me because she wanted to talk to me. When she couldn't find me, she had gone back to the edge of the woods to wait for me there.

It had been four years since the Christmas gift fiasco, and during that time she had not spoken to me, always looking the other way if we should pass each other in school, the store, or on the street. I asked her what she wanted to talk to me about, and she said that she had heard from my sister how embarrassed I was when she had given me the billfold and that she was sorry it had happened but could never get up enough courage to tell me so until now. We stood there and talked for a little while. She told me she really liked the candle stick holders and the red candles (that my mother had forced me to take to her as a return gift.) She said her mother had used them on their Christmas dinner table. I told her I still had the billfold and that it was the first one I ever had; it still had Greer Garson's picture in it. What I didn't tell her was that I used it in my right hip pocket as a sliding pad when I played baseball.

She said she should get home, since it was getting late. Suddenly, she kissed me on the cheek and turned and ran out of the pasture to the road. I had a terrifying thought that what if some of my buddies saw her leaving the pasture and saw me following in the next few minutes. I would never live it down, so I went back to the tree I had been in and climbed up and sat on the limb for a while before coming down and walking to the other side of the pasture next to the railroad, taking the back way home.

My mother was standing on the front porch looking for me, asking where I had been and what I'd been doing. I told her I had been over in Moore's Pasture to spot us a Christmas tree, so that when the time came to go and cut one, it would already be picked out.

HULA GIRL

She would go to the post office every day looking for a letter from her boyfriend. Some weeks she would only get one letter, sometimes two. You could always tell when the letter was from him. She was more friendly than usual to us boys who were often playing a game of tossing a baseball or football in the vacant lot in back of her house. She would walk past us very slowly, holding the letter up to her cheek and lips while singing or humming a song. One of us would get up the courage to ask her, "Are you dancing tonight, Eva?" She would smile and say "Yes, I will be dancing tonight."

She was eighteen and we were all around five or six years younger and she knew that we watched her dance. Later on that night we knew what the ritual would be. Soon after it got dark, three or four of us boys would gather on the back steps of our house, which backed up to the rear of her house at an angle. We would sit there until she came into her bedroom, walked over to the window facing us, and slowly pull the shade down all the way to the bottom of the window. This was our clue to move from the steps to a spot closer to the window. She would turn on her record player and put the record on the turntable. Hawaiian music began to play. She would come back to the window and raise the shade about four inches, which was our signal to come up to the window to watch the show. She would disappear for a few minutes, then return in only her grass hula skirt which her boyfriend had sent her from Hawaii. She would be holding a large framed picture of her sailor boyfriend, who was on a ship somewhere in the South Pacific, against her breasts, with nothing on under it.

She would do her version of a hula dance for the entire record two or three times. She would never move the picture, even though we lived in hope that she would forget and move it or accidentally drop it. She would dance around the room with her hips swaying to the music, and always end the show by a slow turn facing the window where she knew we were watching and hold the picture with one hand as if she was about to remove it. Then she would reach up with her other hand and take hold of the cord to the ceiling light, simultaneously turning out the light and moving the picture! You can imagine the loud groan from us boys as our hopes fell once again.

One day she came home from the post office carrying a letter, but this time it was not up to her lips or cheek and she was crying. She walked by us and did not speak or even look at us, and went straight into her house and closed the door. We waited on the steps till after dark, but there would be no show that night. As she came into her bedroom and turned the light on, we eased our way over to the window, but all we could hear was sobbing. It seems that her sailor boy had written that he had found a real hula girl to take her place. As she sat on the edge of her bed crying of a broken heart, we cried too! No more shows. And to make things worse, her family moved away one week later.

"BUFFALO GAL"

One day while gathering on the company store steps, the question was brought up among us guys as to which neighborhood church had the most "affectionate" girls. There was a boast that the First Baptist did. One guy whose girlfriend went to Second Baptist said he was sure that church would be the winner. Pretty soon the other guys whose girlfriends went to Riverside Church of God, Collins Memorial Methodist and Riverside Church of the Nazarene were involved in the fray. The argument went on for some time and guys were willing to make wagers on it.

Then the question arose: How could you prove your boast? Suggestions were thrown out for discussion, each more absurd and funny than the last. One of the guys kidded another that he knew his girlfriend could not win because she was previously HIS girlfriend and she certainly was not very "affectionate." Tempers flared and the guys almost came to blows and had to be separated. Finally the rules were laid out as to how the contest would be conducted. It would include five churches, five girls, and six guys. (One guy had no girlfriend at the time and would serve as an impartial judge.) Two of the guys had two girl friends, each one in different churches; however, the girls did not know about each other. These two guys had to choose which girl they wanted to enter in the contest. The judging would take place at the Riverside Theater or any other chosen place. After a series of odd man out by flipping coins, Jack was chosen to be first with his Collins Methodist girlfriend, and the judging would occur at the theater on the following Saturday night. It was decided that the subjects would sit four rows from the back of the theater and the judges (the impartial guy and two others chosen by a coin toss) were to sit two rows behind them so they could see what action was going on.

Jack and his girlfriend showed up, purchased tickets, and went in. In those days, you did not necessarily go to the theatre at the start of the movie. You would just go in and stay until the movie came around to the part that you came in on. The judges showed up and sat two rows directly behind the subjects. They gave the prearranged signal that they were in place by coughing, twice. Jack, knowing he had to prove his case, gingerly put his arm on the back of his girlfriend's seat. A few minutes later he let it drop on to her shoulders, at which time she picked his arm up and took it from around her and placed it in his lap. This was looking very bad for old Jack, so he forcefully placed it back around her and pulled her closer to him. She did not move for a few seconds. Then she was heard to say, "Move your arm," which he did immediately. Jack was now 0 for 2 and striking out was on the horizon. And to make it worse, he was hearing muffled laughter from two rows back. Jack sat still for about ten minutes watching the movie and you could tell he was about to lose it. He suddenly grabbed the surprised girl and turned her face toward him and kissed her.

She jumped up and said "Have you lost your mind?" and her popcorn scattered everywhere. Then she heard the three judges laughing uncontrollably. She recognized them and threw the rest of her popcorn at them. About that time the theater manager came down and asked them to leave, and she went charging out with Jack behind her begging her to wait. The theater manager also asked the three judges to leave because they could not stop laughing!

Jack, of course, did not show up at the meeting the next day. After all the details were told to the group everyone went berserk. When asked who wanted to be next, John and Henry, who both had Nazarene girlfriends and often double-dated, said they both would be next. On Sunday night the Riverside Church of the Nazarene was starting a week-long tent revival on the big vacant lot next to the church. A huge tent had already been set up and they expected big crowds each night. John and Henry said they would be at the meeting on Monday night with their girlfriends and sit on the very back row. They invited all four of the groups to show up as judges. Jack finally showed up on Monday and agreed to go, hoping he would not be the only guy everyone was laughing at. We met at the store and rode up to the church in one car, parked and started toward the big tent. Music was playing and a big crowd had already assembled and people were having to stand around the outside of the tent. We spotted John and Henry and walked up behind them, giving the signal that we were in place. The song leader asked everyone to stand and join in the singing. As they stood, John and Henry put their arms around the girls' waists and pulled them close to them and the girls did not flinch. Points for the Nazarene guys. John and Henry had apparently laid out a plan of action. When the song was over and a prayer was being voiced, both guys kissed their girlfriends, then bowed their heads. Jack could not believe what he was seeing and nudged me and said "Did you see that?" The next move as they sat down was to put their arms around the girls' shoulders and the girls leaned into them. More points for the Nazarene boys. During the next prayer another kiss was exchanged and Jack could not take it anymore and left. No adults were watching these two couples and they continued to act as though no one was around them. Another prayer, another kiss; they were whispering in each other's ears and laughing. A love offering was about to be taken and the ushers were asked to take their posts. One usher showed up from outside the tent and took his post starting on the back row where the two couples were seated. As the prayer preceding the offering was being said, another kiss occurred. They had not noticed this usher standing at the end of their row, and as they looked up he was giving them a look that would melt an iron fence post. He came over behind them and told them not to move, he would be back to talk to them as soon as the offering was over. After he moved on down the aisle, everyone split as fast as they could, expecting a posse of ushers to chase us down.

The next day at the meeting on the store steps, the decision was made by all to forfeit the remainder of the contest to the Nazarene guys. The remaining contestants felt it would be impossible to top what went on under the Nazarene tent. We even made up a song to sing for the winning team to the tune of "Buffalo Gals won't you come out tonight?" It went: " Nazarene girls won't you come out tonight, come out tonight, come out tonight (repeat) and see _____(fill in your own name, as most of the guys did) by the light of the moon." On Wednesday night, Charlie and I went back to the tent meeting for the sole purpose of meeting some Nazarene girls. After the service was over, we were talking with some people we knew when we spotted two girls standing alone and went over and introduced ourselves. Turned out they were the Mauldin sisters, fraternal twins. They were waiting for someone to give them a ride home, but that person was not ready to leave, so we volunteered to take them home, which was about half a mile away. Charlie was driving his daddy's 1939 Ford that looked like it just rolled off the show room floor. His dad took excellent care of the car and dared him to put a scratch on it. One twin got into the front seat with him and the other in the back seat with me, and we were slowly driving them home. They lived at the end of a road with a couple of sharp curves in it. I noticed that Charlie had put his arm around the girl, and I was wondering how he was going to change gears on a stick shift in the floorboard. I don't know what happened next and Charlie would never tell me, but just as we started into the sharp curve, all of a sudden the girl slapped him and he lost control of the car. We jumped a curb and went through the front yard of a house, all of us bouncing all over the car. After running through a row of hedges, he was able to get the car stopped. We all got out and were glad to see that no one was hurt. The twin that was in the front seat with Charlie came over and said something to her sister and they took off running the rest of the way to their home. All Charlie could do was stand there cleaning the hedges off the grill and front end of the car, moaning "O God, O God." I told him he better be praying to God before his daddy sees this car. We finally got all the hedges out from under the car and were able to drive it home. His daddy worked on the second shift and would not get home until 11:45 p.m., and would sleep until about ten-thirty the next morning. I promised to be at his house at sunrise to see if we could get the car fixed up so it would not look damaged, or if it did we were going to make up a story about being run off the road. Fortunately, after we washed it and got the mud off the tires, you could hardly tell there had been any problem unless you looked up under the car where most of the scratches were made by the hedges. Charlie must have prayed hard, because two days later while his daddy had the car at the A&P in Atlanta, someone backed into the front end with a pick-up truck and eliminated all the evidence of the ride through the hedges.

Charlie says to this day that he did nothing to cause the twin to slap him, and in fact he does not even remember this whole story. However, when I see him I start to whistle "Buffalo Gal" and he just grins and turns red.

LINT HEAD

Even though I grew up in a cotton mill village, I had never heard the term "lint head." I didn't know it was a derogatory term used to identify a certain class of people. I guess the folks who worked in the mill never referred to each other by that name. My first encounter with the term came when I was around seventeen. My first cousin, Cynthia, lived in the West End section of Atlanta, and she had a way of giving the impression that people from that area were somehow a superior class. Cynthia told me that one of her girlfriends had expressed an interest in dating me. I had previously met the girl, and was definitely interested, since she was attractive, a varsity cheerleader and apparently quite popular with the high school athletes. Cynthia told me that she had built me and my family up somewhat to her friend, and that I should go along with anything she brought up about the family and not go into any unnecessary details.

I called and made a date with her to go to a basketball game at her school, and afterward to meet my cousin and some other friends of theirs at the local drive-in restaurant. After a long week, Friday evening finally came and I was looking forward to the game and get-together afterward, meeting new people and seeing others I had previously met but not seen in a while. I arrived at her large and rather imposing house about ten minutes early and got out of the car and approached the house not feeling very sure of myself. I had to seriously talk to myself to keep from turning around and leaving. All the way over there I had had a bad feeling things weren't going to go well.

As I approached the front porch, her father was standing there watching me. I spoke to him and he told me to come on in. As I got to the top step he asked me what model of car I was in. I replied it was a 1940 Plymouth. He wanted to know if it was my car or my father's, and I told him it was our family car, the only one we had. He didn't say anything further about the car, but told me to have a seat there on the porch and his daughter would be out shortly. As he and I sat there, he started questioning me about school, sports, and whether I worked part-time. Then he asked how many brothers and sisters I had; then he asked what my father did for a living. I replied that he was a loom fixer in a cotton mill, and had been for years. At that point, he suddenly got up, saying he was going to see what was keeping his daughter. Relieved that he had stopped questioning me, I waited a while and was starting to wonder what was going on. I could hear loud talking coming from inside the house.

Shortly afterward, his daughter came out on the porch and it was evident she had been crying. She told me that her father was not going to let her go out with me, and when I asked why, she said he was very prejudiced in some things and his reason was he would not let her go out with anyone from a family of lint heads, whom he considered low class people.

I called my cousin Cynthia the next day to tell her what happened. She had already heard it from her friend, and tried to laugh about it and said I should forget about it. I told her I didn't like being humiliated, and asked what she had told the girl about my family. She would only say she had led her to believe we were a little "higher class" people than we were, and that she had had no idea that the father would question me.

Needless to say I never let my cousin set me up again - and our relationship was quite distant from that day on.

Since that was the first (but not the last) time I heard the term "lint head," I asked my Dad about it and he explained it was because people working in a cotton mill where spinning, weaving and other projects working with cotton were taking place, the air was usually full of flying lint. After being around it for eight hours your hair and clothes would be covered with lint. This denigrating term became a put-down of some very hard-working people.

By the way, I learned from my cousin a couple of years later that the girl had married a mechanic at a downtown auto dealership. I replied, "Do you mean she married a "grease monkey?" Her response was "no comment."

37 FORD, BULOVA WATCH, AND LOVE

One fall day I ran across a 1937 Ford Coupe that had been sitting in a field behind a barn. I stopped and went to the house and knocked on the front door. An elderly gentleman came to the door and asked if he could help me. I inquired about the Ford behind his barn, was it for sale? He said that he would be willing to part with it, but he wanted me to know that it had not run for several years. He agreed to let me look at it. It looked like the body was in great shape, but all the tires were flat and in various stages of dry rot. I checked to see if it had any oil in it and when I pulled the dip stick out it was like molasses it was so black and thick. The engine looked fairly good, so I asked what he would let it go for and he said he would take forty-five dollars for it as is, with no guarantee that it would ever run. I agreed to pay him the asking price and would return the next day to pay him and get the car. When I told my father about it and what I was paying, he thought I had lost my mind.

The next day a friend went with me in his pickup truck and we had a chain to tow the car with if we could not get it cranked. I took the necessary tools along with fresh gas and new oil, spark plugs, and a new battery and a tire pump.

After spending two hours draining out the old oil, changing the spark plugs, installing the new battery, new gas, and pumping up the tires, we were ready to see if it would crank or whether we would have to pull it with the truck to get it home. We tried several times to get it started but the engine would turn over but would not crank. We then figured that it was not getting any gas, so we decided to prime the carburetor with the fresh gas. After raising the hood and removing the air filter, we poured the gas into the carburetor and waited a couple of minutes before trying it. We figured it would either blow up the engine or start a fire. Upon hitting the starter a flame about two feet high came out of the carburetor, the engine caught and started rattling, then backfired twice with a deafening boom. The muffler had apparently rusted out and it came off and a large black cloud of exhaust engulfed the car. We got a safe distance away just in case the gas tank was next.

The old farmer came running from behind the barn terrified, thinking we had killed ourselves. However, after he saw we were away from the car and okay he started yelling at us, something about the explosion would cause his cow to go dry. After the smoke cleared, the car was running somewhat smoothly. I put the air filter back on, lowered the hood and drove the car off the property and home.

The next day I started to clean the car up. After washing it and using a cleanser that removed the oxidation, the paint was in fairly good shape to be that old. The car looked pretty sharp. I had found four used tires at a service station that would fit and after twenty minutes dickering with the station owner I bought them for $1.50 apiece, including four used tubes that had been patched a few times over.

After a couple of days, Daddy began to feel sorry for me and quit laughing at my car and decided to help me on it. He took out the spark plugs and set the proper gap on them and also bought a new set of points and installed them. After that he cranked up the car and adjusted the carburetor and it ran really smooth. Next, he put on a new exhaust pipe and muffler. After this work was done the car ran like a sewing machine and I drove it on into December. Several guys were wanting to buy it from me, but I told them it was not for sale. Just before Christmas, Junior, one of the guys wanting to buy the car, came to me with a deal on it. He had purchased his girlfriend a diamond Bulova wrist watch for Christmas, but they had broken up, so he wanted to trade me the watch which he had paid $110 for. I told him I did not need the watch, but he kept on begging me to trade with him. He showed me the sales slip to verify the cost, but I still refused. The next day he was back again, telling me how much he wanted that car. I started thinking that watch might be a nice Christmas gift for my mother, who as far as I knew, had never had a watch. Finally I told him I would trade with him, but I had to have fifteen dollars to boot, to which he agreed. So the deal was made on the car. I put the watch, which was in a beautiful velvet lined box, in my dresser drawer, and told my parents I had sold the car.

When I sold the car, it still needed a little work done on it, like one of the headlights was cracked and did not work, and the horn would not blow. On December 20, Junior showed up at my house with the car and seemed upset about something. He got out of the car and said he needed to talk to me. I asked him what the problem was and he wanted to know if I still had the watch. I told him I did and asked why. It seems he had made up with his girlfriend and had to have the watch back, because before they broke up he had shown the watch to a couple of her girlfriends and they had told her what he had her for Christmas. He was desperate to get the watch back. I told him to just go and buy another watch, and he said he didn't have the money and he thought I might be willing to take the Ford back. I had thought the watch would be a nice surprise for my mother, but since he was in such a jam with his girlfriend and needed to save face, agreed to give him the watch and take the car back for fifteen dollars to boot, since I was not sure what shape the car was in since Junior was known to be a reckless driver. He assured me I would find the car in good shape and would gladly give me the fifteen dollars boot.

After I took the car back, I noticed the headlight had been replaced and the horn now worked and the car had four brand new tires. It had also been waxed and shined to such a brilliance I thought it had been painted. I figured my total investment in this car was about $75, and now I had $30 of that back from the two trades and still had the car in better shape than when I bought it. Junior got his girlfriend back and was able to give her the wristwatch she knew she was going to get. Their relationship grew and after high school they got married. As for the Ford, I drove it for two more months and then sold it for $95, using part of the money to buy a 1940 Pontiac Coupe, but that's another story.

SCRAP IRON

When I was around seven or eight years old, I already knew that having some money was important and also that it was scarce around our house. There was no such thing as an allowance and just asking for a nickel to buy candy or a coke was a non-issue. With only one parent working in our family, food and clothing were the number one priorities. I learned that if I was to have any spending money, I would have to figure out a way to earn what I needed.

One day I noticed that there was a man who came around through our village in an old beat-up truck and everyone referred to him as the "rag man." He would purchase old clothes, rags, and scrap metal from people who saved up these materials for him. Even though I had seen him around, it was not until then that I became aware of what he actually did. My Daddy explained to me that he came around about every two weeks and would pay money for these items. He suggested that I could also start making some money the same way.

At some previous Christmas I had gotten a second-hand red wagon, so I started going around the village to see what I could find. If I saw a piece of metal in someone's yard, I would ask if I could have it. In most cases, they gave it to me. During this time period men worked on their own cars and once in a while I would reap a bonanza by being able to pick up a broken axle, tailpipes, old mufflers and sometimes a bent wheel.

I decided to "specialize" in metal only, since the rag man paid by weight only. One day, I was given a tip that if I was willing to dig around in the village dump I could probably find a lot of scrap iron without having to go all over the village, and would not have to ask for it. Since the dump was over behind the baseball field, it was very close for me to get to it. I could go to it most of the time without anyone seeing me. It turned out to be a great source of metal. So about every two weeks or so, I would have a wagon load of metal for the "rag man." As I recall, the going rate was one or two cents a pound, which was not very much considering the work to gather it up. However, it did keep the competition down, as I don't recall any other boy who was doing this to make money. But there were always a couple of friends who were eager to help me spend my hard-earned money at the company store!

Not long after I started this enterprise, a local man who worked in the store where I spent my money hung the name "Scrap Iron" on me, a nickname that is still used by some of my boyhood friends to this day.

PAPER BOY

The best job I had was delivering the Atlanta Journal. I had been helping a friend who had the route covering the area where I lived, and when he decided to give up the job he asked if I would like to take it over. I met with the route supervisor and since I already knew the route, he gave me the job.

My mode of transportation for delivering newspapers was a three-wheel Cushman motor scooter with a box on the front to hold the papers. The gas tank held only two gallons and I was able to fill it up every other week for forty cents. The price of a gallon of gas was twenty cents, which now would buy you a thimble full.

One day my friend Thomas Hales wanted to help me deliver papers, and we decided he would ride in the box. When I started up the steep hill on Tribble Drive from Bolton Road, a main thoroughfare, we were about half-way up the hill when the chain came off and the brake would not hold. We started going backward. Instinctively I jumped off, but Thomas was still in the box as the scooter sped across Bolton Road (fortunately no cars were coming) and off down through the woods he went. This adventure had a happy ending, as he was not injured, nor was my scooter. For some reason, Thomas refused to help me deliver papers any more.

There was another incident involving the scooter which involved a huge Great Dane that belonged to a family in "Larry Town." The first time I drove the scooter down his road he chased me for a little ways and then stopped. The next day when I came down his road he ran toward me and suddenly jumped clear over the box! I stopped the scooter and he came trotting by me and went to his yard and lay down. From then on it became a sort of ritual. The dog would run at me, jump over the box, and go back to his yard and lie down. One day my younger brother Bobby was riding with me to help on the route, and I had not told him about the dog. When we started down the road here came the huge Great Dane as fast as he could run and jumped the box. Bobby ducked into the box and started crying and screaming in fear for his life. After it was over, he went home and told on me to our parents. Lucky for me, they just thought it was funny.

In those days the customers were not satisfied with having their paper thrown on the driveway or in the yard as is done today, but it had to be put on the porch, or in some cases the customer might insist it be put behind their screen door.

You learn a lot about people when you are dealing with them on a daily basis. My customers were all mill workers except two, the Baptist preacher and the Methodist preacher. During those days the Journal was delivered in the afternoon. Being a newspaper boy taught you a lot about business in that you had to pay for every paper on your route, so you had to count your papers when they were brought to your pick-up spot and make sure you had the exact number. I learned a lot about service and collection of my money, which was very trying at times. One customer I had complained that I had missed him on several occasions when I knew that I had not. He worked on the second shift in the mill and had already left for work before I delivered his paper. He would not pay me for the days he said I missed. Since it was happening every once in a while, I felt like something was wrong and suspected someone was stealing his paper. One day I made him my last stop of the day to be sure I had left his paper. I then went around the corner and waited to see if someone was taking the paper. In just a few minutes his neighbor came out and went over to his porch and picked up the paper and left with it. The next day, I went to my customer's house before he left for work and asked him if he got yesterday's paper and he said he did. This was a puzzle to me, when I had seen his next door neighbor get the paper and leave with it. I then explained to my customer what I had seen and that I had to pay for those papers he said he didn't get and how much of my profit was being stolen by his neighbor. He became furious and said he would talk to the man and get it taken care of.

The next day was a Saturday, and that was the day I did most of my collecting. I went out early and when I got to the missing-paper customer he came to the door and paid only for the papers he had received, not for the ones his neighbor had stolen. After he paid me, he told me his neighbor wanted to see me, so I went next door and knocked on the door. He came out on the porch and waved at my customer who was watching from his front porch, who turned and went into his house. The neighbor asked me if I knew how many papers I had not been paid for, and of course I knew exactly the number and told him, and at that point he paid me for them and then asked me if

I would start leaving him a paper each day. I told him I would be glad to. He always paid on time, and sometimes even in advance. One day I asked my original customer what he said to his neighbor. He just laughed and told me he had found out that his neighbor would come over and get the paper when he got off work and read it and then put it back on the porch. However, sometimes he would get busy and forget to bring it back. He apologized to him and also to me, and he made a very good customer.

Another customer I had was an older lady who had asked if I would start leaving her a paper, and I started it the next day. At the end of the first week I went by to collect and she told me she was short on money and could I wait until next week. I agreed, although I knew that would mean I would pay for her paper for two weeks before I could collect. The following Saturday she said she could only pay me twenty cents on her bill, which by this time was up to ninety cents. She promised to catch up the next week. I fell for her promise and took the twenty cents. I was now in the hole seventy cents and by the next week it would be a dollar fifteen, which she promised to pay me in full. On Saturday I went by and she could only pay seventy cents, and if I would stop by on Monday she would catch up. She was a grandmotherly type who seemed very nice. My parents knew her and my father worked with her in the mill. Also, I delivered papers to her two married sons, who always paid on time. So I told her I would be by on Monday. School was out for the summer, so I got up early and right after breakfast I got my bicycle out and rode to her house. I went to the door and knocked, but got no answer. She lived in one side of a duplex, and when I knocked again her neighbor came out and told me she had moved out on Sunday to another state to live with her daughter. I thought about telling her two sons about it but had second thoughts. I learned later she had a grocery bill she skipped out on. Out of 120 customers, she is one of only two to ever beat me out of money.

The other was a strange guy who lived in an odd place to deliver papers. The stop was the old Whittier House that was built in the mid-1800's for the Whittier family that owned the cotton mill. The large house had been turned into several apartments where I had customers. In order to deliver their papers, I had to enter through the huge front door that opened into a large ballroom, and then leave the papers at each customer's door. This was not too bad during the weekdays because it was daylight and usually someone was around or outside. or their apartment door was open. On Sunday mornings, though, it was a different scene. I would be in there around daybreak and it was an eerie feeling as there was only a dim light and no sounds except the creaking of the floors as I walked around the large room, leaving a paper at each door. Over the years a lot of ghost stories had been told about that house. In the big room was a large fireplace with a huge mantle that was around ten feet high and on the mantle sat a large vase that was rumored to contain the elder Mr. Whittier's ashes and that his ghost still resided there. On many a Sunday morning, especially in the wintertime, I could swear I heard a loud moan or cry which would cause me to speed up my delivery. All the customers there were good about paying me every week. Then the state of Georgia instituted a one per cent sales tax which also applied to newspapers. One of my customers who I will refer to as the "old man upstairs," was strange in that he was seldom seen out in public other than going to and from work. I never knew if he had a wife or not as I never saw anyone but him. He only took the paper Monday through Saturday, which cost thirty cents. When I wold go to collect he would barely open the door and stick his hand out and give me three dimes. On the week the sales tax went into effect, it meant he owed me thirty one cents. I knocked on the door and announced who I was; he opened the door a crack and dropped the three dimes in my hand and shut the door. I knocked again on the door and he answered me through the door and asked what I wanted. I told him he owed me a penny for the sales tax. He let me know right away that he was not going to pay me "no damn sales tax" on a paper. I left because I could tell he was very mad, deciding I would let it go until next week. The next Saturday I knocked on his door again and he opened as usual handing me the three dimes. Before he could close the door, I told him he owed me two more cents. He swung the door open wide, which scared me for a moment, and told me he was never going to pay sales tax. I summoned the courage and told him I would stop delivering his paper unless he paid me. He replied that he did not believe I would stop his delivery over a penny a week. Since he only took the paper six days for thirty cents a week, it meant that I only made five cents a week, and since I had to pay the tax for him I was not going to deliver the paper for four cents. I stopped the delivery. I found out later he started the Atlanta Constitution, and I can only guess he did not pay the tax to that boy, either.

There were many good people on my route, some who would invite me to eat with them. One lady would fix me a cup of hot chocolate on Saturdays in the wintertime when I came to collect. These days, you never see your paper boy; all you see is a car that comes by and your paper is thrown in the direction of your house. You mail your payments in for three, six or twelve months in advance. Worst of all, the Atlanta Journal and the Atlanta Constitution are now combined. WHAT A SHAME!

OYSTER STEW CHEF

One of my many jobs was working at the Riverside Cafe. I was hired to come in after school, which was around 3:30, and work till closing, usually 10:30 to 11 p.m. depending on how soon the third shift workers left to go to work.

My job was waiting on tables, washing dishes, and sometimes frying hamburgers and boiling hot dogs or making sandwiches. Some evenings it was necessary to run some teenagers out so that I could clean up and close up. They wanted to stay around playing the juke box and pinball machine, not caring that I had been in there for several hours and needed to get home. Before I could leave, I had to sweep and mop the floor and clean the grill for the next day.

One night I had finished the clean up and made sure everything was ready for the owner who would open at 7:30 a.m. I was locking the door when a guy came up and it was quite evident he was drunk. I tried telling him I was closing up, but he kept insisting he had to have something to eat. So I decided to let him come in and sit down at the counter. He told me he had not eaten all day and asked if I would fix him something. I told him I would and asked what he wanted. He said he would like a bowl of oyster stew and a cup of coffee. I reheated some leftover coffee and poured him a cup and asked him if he wouldn't rather have a hamburger, but he said no, he wanted oyster stew.

I had never made oyster stew and really did not know what to put in it. I had carried it to tables before and knew what it looked like. So I got a pot out and poured milk in it, since I knew it looked white, and then pulled out a large tub of oysters from the refrigerator and put quite a lot of oysters in the milk. Then I put in salt and black pepper, just guessing at the proper amount. Then I remembered that the bowls I had seen had red specks in it, so I figured it must be red pepper. I looked all over the kitchen and finally found some red pepper and put an extra generous helping in the pot, put it on the stove and let it come to a boil for several minutes. He asked for more coffee and I brought it to him and poured up his oyster stew into a bowl and handed him a spoon. Even though it was still very hot, he dug into it like a starving man and never said another word until he had finished the whole bowl.

When he finally stood up he seemed to have sobered up. He said that was the best oyster stew he ever had and he would come back again. He asked what he owed me, and I told him thirty cents for the stew and five cents for the coffee. He handed me a five dollar bill and told me to keep the change and walked out the door.

I stood there stunned for a moment. Wow! A four dollar and sixty-five cent tip! That was tremendous since I only made ten dollars a week for all those hours I put in Monday through Friday. I looked for him for two or three weeks to come back for more of that great oyster stew, but he never came. I figured that he had totally sobered up and could not remember where he had been that night, or else the stew had destroyed his taste buds.

PIN BALL ALLEY

As I grew older, other jobs came my way, as they usually do if you are looking for ways to earn money.

One that came my way was working at the Riverside Bowling Alley setting up pins. This was not one of my favorites, as it was extremely hot work and had a degree of danger to it. Some bowlers would deliberately roll a ball before you had time to clear the alley and jump up on the back of the lane. Sometimes the beer drinking crowd would come in to bowl and having had one beer too many they would delight and make sport of how many times they could get a pin to fly up and hit the pin boy. They would make bets on who could hit the pin boy with the most pins at one time.

One night a crew of them came in to bowl and as my luck would have it my two lanes were free. It started out fine, as they were bowling against each other and giving me time to get all the pins set and clear the lane with no problem. As the evening went on, though, they became more intoxicated and loud. The manager came over and talked to them and they calmed down for a while. Then all of a sudden it seemed like

115

they all went nuts at the same time. They started rolling balls at a fast pace; before the first ball got to the pins, two other balls were thrown by two other guys. Then they began throwing cross lane balls, pins began flying everywhere, and I could not get out of their way. Several pins hit me on the legs and back. As I got down on the lane, they started laughing and yelling at me to set the pins up again. I picked up several pins in my arms and started throwing them at the drunken idiots and was landing some of them on their backs and arms as they were trying to dodge them, all the time yelling and cursing at me. The manager came running over and escorted them all out of the building and ordered them to leave the premises or he would call the police.

After they left I picked up my game sheets for all the games I had worked and took them to the manager for my pay for the night. He asked me to finish out the night as he had no one to work my two lanes. I told him that my career as a pin setter was over, he paid me and I left. I went back there from time to time, but only as one rolling the balls, not dodging them.

MILL WORKER

During my sixteenth year, I made the decision that I was ready to quit school and go to work in the Cotton Mill. I reasoned that school was a waste of time. After all, a lot of the guys in the village had already quit when they became sixteen and become mill workers. I saw them as being able to have money to buy what they wanted, such as a car or a fishing boat, among other things. Money was hard to come by for the young teenagers in the village unless they had some kind of work to do. The parents in most cases had none to spare, stretched to the limit just to provide the basics for their families. So in the year that I was to turn sixteen I told my parents my plans, that I would not be going back to school in September. My parents, both of whom had only eighth grade educations, said nothing except to ask me if I was sure I wanted to quit school. I told them I was sure.

July, my birth month, was approaching when Daddy told me there was a temporary opening on the second shift in his area, and I could go ahead and start if I was ready. The job was in the weave shop filling batteries on the large looms. Although

I had no idea what the job entailed, I jumped at the opportunity. I was to come in the next day at 3:30 in the afternoon for my training session. I had never been in the part of the Mill where the weave shop was located before, and did not know what to expect. First of all, the noise was so loud my trainer had to get very close to my ear and talk really loud for me to hear. The second thing I realized was that the heat was unbearable. I was told that the heat and humidity had to be kept high in order for the looms to run. The third thing I learned was that a battery was a large metal wheel-like thing that held twenty spools of thread, and as one spool became empty a new spool would drop into the shuttle and the weaving continued without a stop in the process. The fourth thing I learned was that I would be assigned a stand of twelve looms and that I had to make sure I did not let the battery run out of spools of thread. If that happened, the loom would shut down. And if that happened, the fifth thing I would learn is that I would reap the wrath of the weaver on my stand of looms, as they worked on piece time, and if the loom shut down it would cost them money. Sometimes it could take an hour or more to get a loom running again, and the weaver would not be pleased at all.

After two days of instruction, I was to be on my own the next day on the second shift. As I walked in to find my stand, I realized that the weaver was a woman who was known in the village as a person who could lay a few expletives on you at the drop of a hat. She had been known to beat up her husband on several occasions. At 3:30 I relieved the first shift worker with my cart full of spools of thread and started going down the aisle filling in the empty slots on the batteries as I went. I was thinking this is not going to be hard at all. As I got to loom number twelve, I looked back up the aisle to loom number one just as the next to last spool had just dropped into the shuttle. I had to race with my heavy cart back to number one and start filling every vacant slot I could and go all the way down the line doing the same. When I would get to the last one, it would start all over again. I was told I was too slow in getting the spools in the slots, so I was shown how to do it faster and pick up speed in order to stay somewhat ahead of the loom. And this was to go on over and over until 11:30 at night! At 7:30 a relief person would come by and let me take a fifteen minute break in which I had to run to the restroom and also eat my supper, usually one or two sandwiches.

The next morning I realized that the way I was pulling the end of the thread off the spool to wrap it around the battery head had cut into my fingers like razor blades. My hands were so sore I could hardly close them. After the second day on my own I was able to do better. However, on the third day, due to the heat and humidity, my upper body broke out in a heat rash which was the worst pain I had ever experienced and it lasted for three or four days. On the next Saturday afternoon, I was to play in a baseball game. In those days, the uniforms were wool. I was catcher in the game and in the fourth inning, due to the heat of the sun, the wool uniform, and the heat rash, I passed out. I came very close to having a heat stroke, but fortunately I was given the proper treatment and revived.

Monday rolled around, and it was time to go back to work, which I now dreaded the thought of. However, I was determined not to be a quitter, and not to let Daddy know how I felt. This went on into the second week and I kept making myself go in to work day after day. Three weeks went by, seeming like three months. I now had a little money, but I started to wonder if it was worth it and if this was what I wanted to do for the next twenty or thirty years, as some of the mill workers had done. I started thinking about joining the service at one point; I had an uncle who was in the Navy and he was pressing me to finish high school and join with him in the Navy. I just had to figure out a way to quit the Mill and still save face.

On Friday, the end of the third week, Mr. Butler, Daddy's boss, came up to me right before I started my shift and said that he hated to tell me, but the person I had been filling in for was now well and ready to come back to work. So that night would be my last shift. He thanked me for the job I had done. Of course I had to act disappointed, and told him I appreciated the opportunity. On the inside I was jumping for joy! That last night I zipped up and down that aisle faster than I ever had, knowing it was my last night forever on that job and I was not going to allow a loom to shut down. I wanted to leave with the knowledge that I never let it happen for three weeks straight. As I left that night to go meet Daddy to walk home, I saw him standing with Mr. Butler. They were talking and laughing about something, but stopped as I approached them. Mr. Butler shook my hand and told me he would call me if anything came open in the next few weeks, since he understood I wanted to go to work there on a full time basis. I thanked him and told him I would appreciate that.

That night I slept like a dead person on into late Saturday morning. As I got up and started to the bathroom, my parents were talking in the kitchen, and I heard Mama ask Daddy if he thought it worked. He replied that he was sure it did. It suddenly hit me that I had been had. Daddy had talked his boss into letting me work to get an idea of how hard it was in that mill in order to keep me from quitting school. And it worked!

When I confronted him about his scheme, he would not answer me, he just grinned. Needless to say I never mentioned quitting school again. When Mama asked me what I was going to do with the money I had earned, I told her I was going to buy me some school clothes.

TORCHING AUTOS

One job I had was back in the scrap iron business. My Daddy and a friend of his who also worked in the cotton mill came up with the idea of buying junk cars and selling them for the parts and metal. They would ride around through the different areas in which the people living there usually drove older cars and trucks. When something happened to their car that was not repairable or would cost more than the car was worth to fix, they would just park the car and be willing to sell it for junk.

The two auto parts tycoons would ride around and locate a car that they could tell had been parked for a long time. They would approach the owner and offer anywhere from ten to twenty dollars. In lots of cases, they were given the car or truck just to get it hauled off the premises. My Daddy's partner lived in a mill house that was at the end of a dirt road (no paving had reached the village yet) where they were able to build a large timber frame and attach a hoist that would enable them to pull the engines from the cars so they could take them apart. Once they had taken all the parts from the engine, they would clean them to be sold to local used parts stores in the area. After doing that they would move the car back to a clearing where they removed the wheels and axles and drive shaft and leave just the body on the ground for me to do my job.

First, I would break out all the windows, windshield and back window, then soak the seats, which were usually old horsehair, and the headliner with kerosene. Then I would take an old cloth, roll it into a ball, and light it and move back and toss it through the windshield opening and let it burn. After the car had cooled, I would pull the steel coil springs in the seats and lay them aside. I would then take the torch and start cutting it up into pieces to be stacked on a flat bed truck and taken to the junk yard for sale. All the wheels, axles, springs and other usable parts went to the used parts store.

Now, some sixty years later, when I go to classic car shows and I see all these beautiful old cars restored to unbelievable condition worth thousands of dollars, I think about all the Fords, Chevrolets, Cadillacs, and LaSalles (and one I really hated to cut up - a Hupmobile), it brings tears to my eyes.

B & B GAME PRESERVE

My Dad was always looking for ways to supplement his meager wages from the Cotton Mill, and there were many of them. Probably the most far-fetched was his attempt to establish a bird hunting preserve. He and his boss in the mill, Mr. Butler, hatched this idea along with Daddy's previous partner in the car parts business, Mr. Crawford. Mr. Crawford had a few years earlier purchased a 120 acre farm in Hiram, Georgia, and his contribution to this venture was the use of his farm for the preserve.

The three of them made big plans for how they were going to stock the place with many different kinds of game birds. Since they had seven bird dogs between them, they could also become hunting guides and be able to charge an extra price for their services and the use of the seven finest bird dogs in the State of Georgia.

They discussed over and over the type of birds they would get and what their hunting fees would run. It seemed as though they would never agree on the type of stock they would go with. They all had agreed on quail, but they felt they also had to come up with some exotic bird that was not commonly found in Georgia. They felt that if they could come up with something special, they could attract the "rich" hunter around Atlanta and beyond. They discussed turkey, pheasant, and wild ducks and geese since there was a big lake on the property. They checked out various markets for buying their stock. One magazine article they read went on at great length about the excitement of hunting Japanese pheasant, which was reported to be one of the fastest birds off the ground and would be a challenge for any hunter. They were also very good on the dinner table. At last they decided to go with the quail and Japanese pheasant for the first year and expand to other game over the coming years.

They got busy putting up "Posted" signs over the entire farm, and got flyers printed up to pass out to hunters. They knew that normally you should start the stocking process by buying birds and letting them grow and multiply for at least a season, but being impatient and fearing someone else might beat them to opening the first game preserve in the area, they decided to go with older stock, since the hunting season was only a few months away. Through a magazine they had found a supplier that claimed to have the finest bird stock in America. They put in an order for one hundred quail and, because the Japanese pheasant were so expensive, they only ordered twenty-five of them.

The big day came for the arrival of the birds. They arrived late in the evening, so plans were made to leave the next morning around 7 a.m. for the farm. I asked if I could go along and help and was allowed to go. Upon arriving at the farm, the men made a decision to release the quail on one side of the hundred acres and the pheasant on the other side, to keep them apart. Upon reaching the spot where the quail were to be released, they took a crate off the truck and released about twenty-five of them. They did not attempt to fly away, but just walked around exploring their new home. We spread each crate out about fifty yards apart and they all reacted the same way. I guess that since they had been raised in confinement, they thought they still were.

We marked the spot of release and got back in the truck and headed for the side of the farm for the release of the Japanese pheasants. As we unloaded them, they seemed to be fairly large birds to me, but never having seen one, I was not sure how big they were supposed to get. As we took them out of the cages, they reacted just like the quail, wandering around looking for food. The four of us were just standing there watching them and Daddy and his two partners were making big plans and discussing the rates they would charge and really enjoying their vision of coming success as the only game preserve owners in the area.

We noticed all the birds seemed to start gathering in one spot about ten yards away from where we were standing, when all of a sudden as if on cue all twenty-five of the Japanese pheasants took flight, apparently heading for the Land of the Rising Sun from whence their ancestors came!

The big game preserve owners not only saw their birds flying away but the hard earned dollars they had invested in them.

Word got out at the mill about the birds taking flight, and for a while the partners lived a hard life as the kidding was constantly bombarding them. For several weeks they were known as the Sayonara Three. Pretty soon the preserve signs came down, as no one was willing to pay to hunt quail, since they were plentiful in the area on open land for free. I did get to enjoy hunting on the quail farm as it was now called, with my Dad and his friends, and with Ike and Sal, his excellent bird dogs.

CADDY TO THE RICH
AND CHEAP

One day I ventured up to the clubhouse on the company golf course. It was on a weekday when no one was playing. I hung around for a few minutes talking to the clubhouse manager, and just as I started to leave, one of the biggest Cadillacs I had ever seen pulled in to the parking lot. A man got out of the car dressed in a business suit and tie. I was standing there watching him take off his coat and tie and change into his golf shoes and get out his golf bag, when he asked me if I would like to caddy for him. I was not quite sure that I wanted to, but when I looked at his bag I saw that it contained only four clubs, a driver, two irons and a putter, I said I would, since I saw it would not be all that heavy. I envisioned a nice reward at the end of his game. After all, he was well dressed and drove a big fancy car, so he was bound to be rich. It would be easy money!

When he had teed off on the first hole, he took off in a stride that I had to trot just to keep up with. After about the third hole, I figured out this was not a guy who came for a leisurely game of golf. He would hit a bad shot into the woods or slice one over into the other fairways, but would not go look for the balls or allow me to do it. This went on for the entire nine holes. He would hit the ball and take off, throwing the club in my direction to pick up and put in the bag.

By the time we had finally finished the nine holes I was totally exhausted from trying to keep up with him. We walked over to his car, he opened the trunk and I set his clubs in the car and handed him his dress shoes, which he changed into. As he opened his car door and started to leave, he said "Thanks, kid, for caddying for me," and handed me a quarter. As I stood there stunned, looking at the coin, he drove off in his big expensive car back toward the rich side of town, taking my dream of a good payday with him.

After Mr. Rich Guy left, I decided to go into the clubhouse and try my luck with the gumball machine. It was always filled with red gum balls with a few speckled balls mixed in. If you were lucky enough to get a speckled ball, it was worth a nickel. Mr. Helton, who ran the shop, had just filled the machine, putting in a handful of speckled balls and mixing them up a little. I could see that none of them had got to the bottom of the machine, so when Mr. Helton stepped outside for a few minutes, I picked up the machine and gave it a good shake to increase my chances of getting a speckled ball. Since I was tired and thirsty from the fast-paced golf game with the cheapskate rich guy, I bought me a Coke for five cents and asked for five pennies from my change for the quarter to put in the gumball machine. We kids had learned that if you jiggled the lever when inserting the penny, sometimes you would get two gumballs instead of one. I put in my penny and jiggled the lever, but only got one red ball. On the next penny, I hit the jackpot and got two speckled balls. The next penny reaped one red and one speckled, but unfortunately the next two pennies resulted in only two red balls. I cashed in my three speckled balls for fifteen cents and asked for five more pennies.

Mr. Helton gave me the money but stood there watching me. I finished my Coke and started to play again. He saw me jiggle the lever and told me to stop doing that, and I did and got only one red ball. I put in the next penny and out came a speckled ball. I could see Mr. Helton was getting irritated at me, and when I put in the next penny, out came two more speckled balls! He grabbed the machine and would not let me play any more. I cashed in my speckled balls and went outside and sat down on a bench and started trying to add up how much money I had made today. As I sat there, I suddenly remembered the balls that Mr. Hot Shot had hit into the rough and the woods. I got up from the bench and started walking the course again, mentally mapping out where he had hit those balls.

On the second tee, he had sliced a drive real bad, so I walked to that tee and tried to measure in my mind about how far it went, then took off on a line to where I thought it might be. Sure enough, I found it without any trouble. It had cleared a rough area and was lying in a small clearing. He could easily have played the ball if he had only taken the time to look for it. On the fourth tee, he sliced another ball over on the adjoining fairway, very visible, but again he refused to go over and play it. The eighth hole was a very short par three. On his first shot, he drove the ball way over the green into the woods behind. He decided to hit another tee shot and did the very same thing, over the green and into the woods. After a few choice curse words, he had laid the third ball down on the tee and this time used his iron instead of the driver, and he landed this shot within about five feet of the hole. He was very pleased with himself on that shot and sank the very short putt. Again, he would not go look for the first two balls.

It took me about twenty-five minutes of walking in the woods, but I located both balls. As I walked out I spotted another ball, apparently lost by another golfer previously. I now had five almost-new golf balls. The club manager would buy balls that we would find while playing on the golf course if they were somewhat new and not cut up. I took the balls and walked back to the clubhouse to see if Mr. Helton would buy the balls. I figured he was tired of giving me money and would probably not even let me back inside, but he did and I asked him to buy the five balls. He appeared uninterested at first, but I figured this was his way of getting them for a cheap price. After he looked them over, he offered me fifteen cents for the five. I told him I could probably get more if I waited until some golfers showed up that I could sell them to. Not knowing how long that would be, I let him think about it for a few seconds, then told him that I would take the offer if he would throw in a Baby Ruth candy bar. I took the candy bar, the fifteen cents, and left for home. When I got home, I sat down on the front porch to try to figure out my total take for the day. I started out with nothing, got twenty-five cents for caddying, then from the gum ball machine I got six speckled balls worth a total of thirty cents. I sold five golf balls for fifteen cents for a total of seventy cents. I spent five cents for a Coke and eight cents on the gum ball machine. So for the day I still ended up with five red gum balls, sixty-two cents and a Baby Ruth candy bar.

I shared the gumballs with my brothers and sisters and secretly gave the Baby Ruth candy bar to my mama as it was her favorite. All in all, it had been a good day!

HERO

One day I was walking back home from the company store past the long building that was called "the ark." The ark contained several two-room apartments. (My family had lived in the ark when we first moved to the village, but we had since moved into another house.) As I went around the corner of the building, I heard a woman screaming "Fire, fire!" She ran out her back door, followed by a lot of smoke. Once outside, she suddenly started screaming, "My baby, my baby is in there!"

Since I was a Boy Scout and was always prepared, I without hesitation ran into the burning kitchen, then into the front room and located the baby boy on the floor. As I started back towards the door, two men had come in and were lifting the kerosene stove with two wooden broom sticks and throwing the stove into the yard. I followed them out the door, trying to find the mother to give her her baby. Finally I found her and she came running to me, took her baby and walked away without out saying a word to me.

A warm feeling came over me as I stood there waiting to be congratulated on being a hero. No one came, but I suddenly realized that I had my reward. The warm feeling was coming from the large, moist circle on the front of my shirt. The baby I had risked my life for had wet on me!

FAMILY CARS

Cars were a big thing to teenage boys in the fifties. I had no car of my own until I was almost eighteen. I had to depend on using my Dad's car, which at the time I got my driver's license was a 1940 Plymouth four-door sedan. It was probably the ugliest thing ever to be put on four wheels. We had this car for years, and Daddy would not even talk about getting another one.

When I went to get my drivers license, the State Patrol officer giving me the driving test instructed me to turn around in a driveway that was on the left side of the road. This driveway looked to me like a walkway from the front of the house to the mail box. On each side of it was a brick wall. I told the trooper that it did not look wide enough for a driveway and that the Plymouth was too wide to go between the brick pillars. He insisted that it was indeed a driveway, and told me to pull into it and turn around. As I started to pull into the walkway, both front fenders scraped the pillars. I stopped quick, and he said I was right, it was not a driveway. I backed out to a loud scraping sound, and headed back to the testing office. The officer did not say a word on the drive back, and neither did I. When we pulled into the parking lot, he got out and told me to come inside, that I had passed my test and he would issue my license.

As I came out, Daddy was standing at the car looking at the scrape marks on both fenders. He said that from the looks of the car, I must have failed my test! I showed him my license and explained that I had passed, probably *because* I had wrecked the car. I told him the story of how the trooper had insisted he was right but then had to admit he was wrong. There was no way he was going to turn me down for my license, even though I was probably the only person in the state who wrecked a car while taking a driving test and still passed.

My first car was a 1930 Ford Model A which I had purchased from a Mrs. Bradley who was a customer on my Atlanta Journal paper route. Her husband had bought the car brand new, and since he was a Mill boss and lived close to the Mill, he never drove the car very much. He would drive to the grocery store downtown on Marietta Street and on Sunday afternoon he would drive up the road from their house and his wife would get out and walk back home for her health! Mr. Bradley became ill and was hospitalized for about a week before passing away. Several weeks later, when I stopped by to collect for the Journal, I asked Mrs. Bradley about the car and told her if she decided to sell it I would like to buy it if I could afford the price. After a couple of weeks, her son called me to see if I was still interested, and I told him I was if I could afford the price. He asked me if I thought a hundred and fifty dollars was fair, and I said it was. Daddy let me borrow the money on the promise to pay it back from my earnings from the paper route. The first thing I did was wash and wax it! The car had 29,000 miles on it and still had the original tires. Although it was a 22 year old car, it was in almost new condition, since it had been kept in a garage all those years. The car had one scratch on it and that was on the clover leaf gas gauge where Mr. Bradley would strike his matches to light his pipe.

I had a great time driving that car around. Most of the time my two buddies Max and Slug and I would alternate; one would be the chauffeur and the other two rode in the back seat pretending to be persons of wealth or some dignitary or other. A strange thing about that almost new A-Model was that if I asked a girl out for a date she would not want to go in it, but would rather go in the 1940 Plymouth, which looked terrible and drove worse! And if a buddy and I were double-dating, *his* date would want to know which car we were driving. Figure the reasoning on that one!

I drove the Model-A for over a year, but one day a man saw me out washing it and stopped to look at it, asking if I would like to sell it. I told him I might but I needed to ask my father first, and he said he would call me the next day. I discussed it with Daddy and he suggested I ask $350 for it, but to take no less than $300. The man came back, and I told him I would take $350. He studied the car for a while, and then said, "I have $300 in cash on me right now." So I said yes, you can have it for that.

I still owed my Dad about half of the original $150, so I suggested to him that since the old 1940 Plymouth was now in bad shape, it may be time to get rid of it. (It needed a lot of work; it had been turned over on a mountain in Tennessee, the speedometer was broken at 100,000 miles, and the seat covers were worn out, besides the two front fender creases I had put on it when I got my license.) I gave him the $300, which meant

I would be putting in around $150 toward another car, and he would do the same with what I owed him.

A few days later I came home and in front of the house was a 1949 Ford 2-door, bright red with a V-8 engine, straight shift, white wall tires - and no sign of the Plymouth. (It turned out he had somehow got a fifty dollar trade-in for the bomb.) Since he worked on the second shift, I would have access to the car most weekdays. We agreed I would keep the car clean and he would do the oil changes and lubrication and we would each pay for our own gas.

My Dad was always the type that didn't want any attention called to himself, so I knew he would not want me to put dual exhausts and smitties (glass pack mufflers) on the car. So one day after I had saved up the money I went and had it done without telling him. The next morning he went out to go somewhere in the car, and when I heard it roar to life I figured he would be back in the house in a couple of minutes, but he apparently went on to wherever he was going, and when he came back he asked me what I was thinking. I told him I should have asked, but since the car was half mine, I only put them on my half. He did not think that was funny, but left it at that. A few days later he was gone in the car and I had walked up to the store for something my mother needed. It was around two-thirty or so, close to time for him to go to work. A lot of his friends were sitting on the store steps, waiting for time to walk to the Mill. As I came out of the store I saw the red Ford coming down the hill toward the store wide open in second gear. As he got in front of all the guys, he let off on the gas and the mufflers made a big roar. He just looked at everybody and grinned and went on around the block to our house. The guys were laughing and clapping and they took off walking down by our house to meet him and walk on to work. The next morning I started to say something, but before I could he just said "nice sound" and nothing more was said after that.

Several months later my father decided the two-door Ford was too small for us to travel in as a family, so he wanted to get a bigger, four-door car. He met a guy who had a 1951 Chevrolet 4-door with an automatic Powerglide transmission, and the man liked the 1949 Ford, so they worked out a trade. I was not happy with this deal, but I understood the reason for it. Daddy did let me take the car and put on glass pack mufflers and moon hubcaps and half-moon covers on the headlights. That spruced it up some, but the car did not run fast from a standstill.

One thing we teenage guys did on those hot steamy Friday nights of summer was to bring souped-up cars down to the river bridge on the Bomber Plant Road to see who had the fastest car. This was not a race against each other but a race against the stop watch. Six or seven cars would show up. There would be 1949 and 1950 Oldsmobiles, 1939 and 1940 Fords, and even a 1950 Hudson Hornet – cars that I could only dream about. (I was now stuck with a 1951 Chevrolet Powerglide that could go from 0 to 50 in about three days!) The cars would line up with the front wheels on the edge of the bridge, and at the signal of a flashlight on the other end the driver would take off against the stop watch and the shortest time won. Cars would then be worked on and the winner challenged to come back for another run.

All I could do was watch from the sidelines, knowing there was no use to try with a 1951 Chevy Powerglide, showing on the gear shift L for low range, D for normal drive, and R for reverse. But on one of these nights, some wise guy started taunting me that I was chicken not to even try. He kept egging me on, saying your car looks good, sounds good, but is it any good? Against my better judgment, I decided to give in and see what it would do. I pulled up on the bridge, put it in the low gear. I figured I would have to rev the engine up to get a quick start, so I held my left foot on the brake pedal and revved the engine up as far as I figured it would take, then took my foot off the brake and pushed the gas pedal to the floor board. The car moved about five feet and then I heard a swooshing sound and the car would not move any further. I suddenly had that sick feeling that something bad was wrong. I smelled transmission fluid running under the car. I put it in reverse and it would not move; I put it in drive and it would not move. Of course, everyone was laughing except me. I really felt stupid for having been goaded into doing this, but I could not blame anyone but myself. But I still wanted to get out of the car and catch the guy who had taunted me into it and throw him off the Chattahoochee River Bridge! We finally got my car turned around and a friend pulled his car up behind me and pushed me all the way to the top of the hill that led to my home. I told him I could coast from there, which I did, and turned the car into the driveway and parked it.

The next morning, a Saturday, I knew my parents would be leaving early to drive out to Marietta Street to the A&P to buy groceries. I was still in bed when they went out to the car and got in. Daddy cranked the car and put it in reverse and I could hear the engine rev up, knowing the car would not move. He put it in low and drive without success. I heard him raise the hood, knowing he was checking the fluid in the transmission. I heard the hood slam, and he came into the house, where I was still pretending to be asleep. He asked what I did to the car and

I told him I didn't know – it was fine when I parked it. After he checked and saw the seal was busted, he came back and told me there was no way I could have driven that car home as there was no transmission fluid in it and there was no fluid on the ground where it was parked. I knew I had better tell the truth at that point, and of course I said I knew what a stupid thing I did and that I was sorry.

He wanted to know how much money I had saved up and I told him it was $64. He said he thought that is about what a new seal would cost. He got a neighbor to tow him up to Hayes garage in Riverside and left the car, later presenting me with an estimate for $64, which I got out of my hidden wallet and gave to him.

And so it was that I had the only car, and I was the only driver, that could go from 64 to 0 in no time flat.

AIRPLANE

A new preacher had arrived on the scene at the First Baptist Church along with his wife and teenage son. Most all of the teenagers sat in the balcony of the church, which of course was not where they should be. Most of the time the church would place three or four deacons up there to control the talking, laughing, or whatever mischief was going on.

It was the second Sunday for the new pastor to be preaching, and we had been warned in Sunday School that we should behave or the deacons would carry us straight to our parents after church was over, if not before. We had known the pastor's son only one week and really did not know what to make of him. He seemed to be withdrawn and shy and the word was that he had not wanted to move from Florida to Georgia, especially to a "backward mill town," as he put it. We did not know how to connect with him or even whether we wanted to. Little did we know that after that Sunday we would see him in a new light that would make him one of us.

The church service started. The singing was as usual and the offering was about to be taken. After that, the choir would sing the special music, the pastor would pray, and then begin his sermon for the day. During the offering, I noticed the preacher's son, who was sitting on the row in front of us, using the church bulletin to make a paper airplane, one that would have a sharp pointed nose and wide wings, very aerodynamic. I thought to myself, this can't be good if he is going to do what I think he is going to do.

Sure enough, the pastor stood up and asked everyone to bow their heads to pray. Just as everyone except the few of us who were now watching his son bowed their heads, he launched the plane, which took off and went over the right side of the balcony. Somehow it made a short circle and the air conditioning vent caught it and blew it back to the front of the balcony; it made two circles over the two front rows of the balcony, barely missing a deacon's head. Unfortunately, the pastor's prayer was very short, something on the order of "bless the preaching of Your Word." Just as he looked up, the plane had finished its last circle, going over the front of the balcony headed straight down the center aisle towards the pulpit. It was still high in the air when the pastor started preaching and he didn't miss a beat even though he was about to get hit by an airplane.

By this time, every teenager in the balcony saw it and were about to die trying to hold back the laughter. The deacons were standing up with faces white as a sheet one minute and red as a beet the next. About three-quarters of the way down the center aisle, the plane made a sharp bank to the left and began a series of circles, going from about half-way down to back up to the ceiling. The choir had caught sight of the runaway plane, half of them looking on in horror and the other half about to break up laughing.

144

Just as the air-conditioning, which was keeping the plane airborne, shut off, the plane started to descend in shorter circles, getting ready to land - somewhere. Right under its landing pattern sat a big lady who was known for wearing big hats to church, and this Sunday morning was no exception. This hat was as big as a Mexican sombrero and had several long multi-colored feathers on it. No one around her had noticed the plane yet. The pastor was staring up at the balcony, at the same time trying to retain his composure. The deacons were praying that the air-conditioning would come back on and put the plane on a different course, to no avail. It made one last circle, landing softly on the feathers of the hat. We waited for the lady to scream, but she never moved, continuing to concentrate on the pastor's words. A man sitting behind her gently lifted the plane off her hat, wadded it up and stuck it in his pocket. The pastor continued his sermon for a few more minutes as things got back to normal as possible, but cut it short and asked the choir to sing the invitation hymn, which hardly any of them could do with a straight face.

As soon as the benediction was said, the deacons in the balcony blocked off the exits and would not let any of us out. They said no one could leave until the guilty one confessed. All us teenagers agreed that our heads were bowed and we did not see the plane until it was airborne. Then the pastor and choir director both came up into the balcony where we were being held and the pastor gave us a short sermon on how we should behave in church, and until we proved we could do it, the balcony would be off-limits to all young people. He went on to say that he understood our wanting to protect the guilty person, but that he knew who it was and he would deal with that individual later on.

We found out later that his son had pulled the same stunt in the two previous churches they had served in Florida. That just gave the him even more status, and we knew then that our new preacher's son was one of us.

THE TROTLINE

One day my good friend "Two-weeks" Evans and I were out just fooling around when he suggested we walk down to the Chattahoochee River. We got to the bank of the river down behind the Cotton Mill and started walking upstream toward the main highway (Bomber Plant Road) that crossed the river at about a mile from where we started. As we approached the bridge, we noticed a commotion out in the middle of the river and realized that it was a trotline that someone had put out. A trotline is a long piece of steel cable or rope that is tied to trees on either side of the river, with fishing line tied to the cable at intervals of several feet with fish hooks attached. Each hook is baited with worms, liver, or any other type bait that would attract the fish. We noticed that the line was really jumping on the water, and figured it had to have a world-record catfish hooked somewhere toward the middle of the river.

Most of the men who fished there left their boats in the river, tied to trees along the bank. We found one that had a small chain around the tree that was easily released. We "borrowed" the boat, along with the oars, and proceeded to row out to see what was hooked. We lifted the trotline out of the water and started down the line pulling up the hooks to see what was there. The first three lines had small perch, crappie, or catfish, but we still hadn't pulled out that "world's record." As we moved on further up the line, we suddenly felt the weight of something big. We had pulled up on the trotline to get the boat under it to give us more leverage, when the largest turtle we had ever seen surfaced and before we knew it he was half in our boat and half in the water! He was so big and so heavy he was about the capsize the boat! "Two-weeks" was seated right where he was trying to get into the boat, and he panicked and started screaming for me to back the boat up. I tried, but it would not move because we were under the trotline.

"Two-weeks" then grabbed one of the oars and started trying to knock the turtle off the side, and when he hit him he broke the line the turtle was hooked on, which allowed the monster freedom to come further into the boat. I yelled at him to knock him off and he kept hitting at the turtle, and finally with one last mighty swing he caught him with a solid blow that broke the oar but knocked the turtle into the water.

The Chattahoochee at that time was very wild. No dams had been built to control it. With the one oar we had left, we attempted to get back to the bank, but were caught in an undertow that started us going around in circles. We could not get out of the current and we were being carried further and further down river. Finally, the current calmed and with the one oar we were able to get to the bank. We had been carried about a mile downstream from where we "borrowed" the boat. After getting the boat on land, we realized we were now faced with a difficult decision. We could set the boat adrift and never say anything about it, letting the owner believe it was stolen and abandoned, or we could start walking along the bank, pulling the boat back up river.

We decided the honest thing to do was to pull the boat back up river. To accomplish this, we had to pass the chain around bushes and trees (sometimes finding ourselves falling into the edge of the water.) After almost two hours of tiring physical labor, we finally got the boat back to the tree it was chained to. We carefully wrapped the chain around the tree so that it looked like it had never been moved, and placed the oar in the bottom of the boat. Then we casually walked away as if nothing happened.

We were never able to tell anyone about our encounter with the monster turtle of the Chattahoochee. And we never heard of anyone talking about a missing oar. We walked by the river many times after that, but when we saw a trotline splashing in the water, we would always wonder if he was back. But we only wondered for a moment --then we just kept on walking.

STORM WARNING

One hot and humid day in August, my parents were going to the A & P Grocery Store on Marietta Street in Atlanta. I was given several chores to do while they were gone, and was warned not to go anywhere until I had the chores done. After they had left and I was starting to do the work, five of my friends came by on their way to the creek to go swimming, and wanted me to go with them. I explained to them I had to get these jobs done or I would be in big trouble. They said we would be back before my parents got back and then they would help me with my chores. I took off with them, knowing full well that it would be impossible for me to get back and also knowing that it seemed that every time I disobeyed my mother something bad happened to me.

We got to the creek and were having a good time swimming and playing games and not paying any attention to the huge black clouds forming in the distance. We started to hear thunder, but it didn't sound close, and the spot where we were swimming was still in bright sunshine. We continued to enjoy ourselves. Several minutes later we could tell the storm was getting closer, but still we ignored it and continued our play.

All of a sudden it was as if somebody opened a flood gate. We saw a huge wall of water rushing towards us, quickly becoming a raging river carrying all kinds of debris with it. We could tell it was going to be over our heads. We scattered to the closest bank to get to higher ground. For three of us it was the wrong bank, as our clothes were on the other side with the other boys. We could not get to our clothes except by walking up to the road and crossing over the bridge. The road was about seventy yards away , and all this distance we would be walking naked. We would only be on the main road for about five minutes, but we would be out in the open field walking up to the bridge and walking back down to our clothes. We were sure to be seen.

One of the guys on the side where our clothes were had an idea. Years ago someone had strung two cables across the creek, one cable to walk on and one to hold on to if you were tall enough to reach it. None of the three of us was tall enough to cross over on the cable, so the tallest guy on the other side told us to stay put and he would bring our clothes over to us. He gathered up three pairs of overalls and three shirts and climbed up on the cable to start over the still raging creek. In a few minutes I would be putting on my clothes and getting up to the road and home before my parents got there!

Everything was going fine until he was two-thirds of the way across - almost to the bank - and he lost his balance and fell about twenty feet into the creek, along with our clothes. We could just imagine our clothes rushing down the creek into the Chattahoochee River. He went under as he hit the water and finally surfaced a little way down the creek and we ran down to him, still naked, and pulled him out. To our great surprise and relief, he was still holding on to our clothes. I quickly put on my clothes and started running for home as fast as I could, all the time trying to think up a good excuse as to why my clothes were wet and muddy.

Somehow my parents were not home yet, so I got real busy doing my chores with my clothes drying on me, wondering why every single time I did something I was not supposed to do, I paid for it. By the time I had finished, my clothes had dried on me and my parents came driving up. They told me they would have been home earlier but they got stranded in the A & P for over an hour because of a REALLY BAD THUNDERSTORM!

THE PREACHER'S ORCHARD

In one of our houses lived a bi-vocational preacher. Out behind his house and garage was a large apple tree that was always loaded with apples in the late summer. He also had fig trees, plum bushes and a pear tree.

It was always a great temptation for us guys to raid his orchard, and a battle of wits for us to try to figure out whether the Preacher was hiding out in his garage, in the house, or if he wasn't home, what time he would be home from work. As I think back on it now, I believe he enjoyed making a game of trying to catch us in the act of stealing his fruit, as I don't actually know if anyone ever got caught.

One day my buddy Two Weeks and I were up on the Preacher's garage which was under the big apple tree, and we had filled our pockets with apples. I had already jumped off the roof and was waiting for him to jump, but he froze and could not jump. After several attempts to encourage him to jump, I realized that he was never going to jump. I told him to go back to the tree that we climbed up on and see if he could get down that way, but you had to make a short jump over to a tree limb in order to get down that way. He went over to the tree but he could not jump to the limb. I knew it wasn't long until the Preacher would be coming home from the mill, and I had to figure out a way to get him down. I told him to come back to the low side of the garage and try again.

After a few more attempts to get him to jump without success, I suddenly pretended to look around the side of the garage and yelled at him that the Preacher was coming with his shotgun, and started to run. Now Two Weeks was not known as one of the fastest boys in the village. As a matter of fact I had beaten him in a race earlier in the day by a good twenty yards. But when he leapt off the garage he hit the ground running and passed me in no time flat. After we had stopped running and I told him the truth, he started chasing me and throwing his apples at me. We had a good laugh about the whole thing, and I shared my apples with him as a good buddy should. He swore that he would get even with me sometime when I was not expecting it.

About three weeks later I was at his house to play, and he came down with the mumps the next week. When I came down with them, too, he felt he had his revenge.

ROLL YOUR OWN

On July 5, 1946, the day after Independence Day, I decided it was time to declare my own independence. After all, it was my twelfth birthday. The way I decided to express this new freedom was to roll my own cigarette and smoke for the first time in my life. All my buddies had been smoking for at least a year and some of them even longer.

None of us had the money to buy tobacco, so we harvested our own by picking up cigarette butts from the ground where they had been tossed by the mill workers who gathered on the steps of the company store waiting for time to go to work. We would wait until they had left and then gather the butts (they were called ducks back then) and peel the paper from them and put the tobacco in either a Prince Albert can or a cloth (Duke) bag, whatever your choice was. Mine was the red Prince Albert can. The company store was one of the main focal points of the Mill Village for the male workers, as well as all the boys growing up there. The men who worked on the second shift would gather there around two o'clock before their shift started at three-thirty, usually to try to outdo each other with their tales of the biggest fish caught or in hunting season who shot the most birds, rabbits, or squirrels, and how far away they were when they fired their shots (Sgt. York, Dan'l Boone, or Annie Oakley would not have had a chance with these marksmen); the baseball games they played in as teenagers (home runs traveled farther than current major leaguers, batting averages were higher, and the pitchers among them boasted wins that would put them in the Baseball Hall of Fame.) When their group would leave to go to the Mill, the first shift would get off at three-thirty and assume their places on the steps for an hour or two before going home. The third shift would get off at seven-thirty and continue the ritual, each shift having their own tall tales and accomplishments. These men worked hard and long hours for by today's standards very meager wages, and no one begrudged them these small pleasures.

The Mill whistle had blown signaling the start of the second shift and I knew that Daddy was now at work. I went to the rear of the house and sat down behind a bush so that no one could see me and pulled out my Prince Albert tobacco can and my pack of cigarette papers and began trying to roll my own cigarette. After about three tries, I was able to get it to hold together and bear some semblance to a real cigarette. I had taken three or four matches from the match box on our kitchen stove and was now ready to take my first step toward manhood by smoking my first cigarette. I struck a match on a rock close by and lit the end of the cigarette and ever so gently took a draw and filled my mouth with the smoke. As I did so, I suddenly had the sense that someone was standing off to my side watching as I released the smoke from my mouth, and as I turned around, there stood my father, who had come home from his job because he had forgotten one of his tools.

(He was a loom fixer in the mill and he had to furnish his own tools for his job.) I had never known of a time when he had left for work and forgotten his tools. His forgetfulness and my experiment with tobacco were about to collide.

As he stood there looking down at me, he asked what I thought I was doing. To defend myself, I went into great detail about how all my buddies were smoking and how they had been daring me and calling me a sissy because I would not join them in this rite of passage. I used every excuse I could think of and blamed every one of the guys, but he did not believe it was a good enough excuse since none of them were there twisting my arm to make me do it. He wanted to know where I got the tobacco, and I knew at this point there was no need in digging the hole I was in any deeper. So I explained to him how I came to have a Prince Albert can full of tobacco.

He told me to stand up and put out the cigarette, which I did, as he slowly removed his belt and stood there for a long time thinking about something (I hoped he was talking himself out of using the belt on me). Then he said that he was not punishing me for having caught me smoking, but for the way I had obtained the tobacco. He pointed out to me that there was no telling what kind of germs or disease I could pick up (back then TB was still very common) and that since he smoked, he could not ask me not to, but if I wanted to he would buy the cigarettes for me. After that, he proceeded to give me several good licks with the belt, which left a very strong impression on my mind as well as my rear end. After the lecture and the licking, I lost my desire for cigarettes. I did, however, experiment later on with a cigar and with Beech-Nut Chewing Tobacco, but I will save that for another story.

The one luxury Daddy allowed himself was "store-bought" cigarettes. I never told my buddies that I could have had "store-bought" instead of "roll-your-own." They would have killed me for not taking him up on it, since they could have helped me smoke them. Incidentally, about six months after this happened, one of the men who met on the store steps to smoke was admitted to the TB hospital in Rome, Georgia. He was there for over a year.

REQUIEM FOR BYGONE DAYS

The ballfield is now gone. When the mill owners decided to sell the houses to the tenants, some of the houses had to be moved onto the ballfield to equal out the lot sizes.

The golf course is now filled with residential housing all the way from Parrott Avenue to the Chattahoochee River.

The old Company Store building still exists, bought by an investor and converted to apartments.

The "Ark" likewise has been purchased and converted to apartments.

Moore's Pasture, the place of many of our games, is now covered with huge gasoline storage tanks.

The former site of the village dump now contains homes ranging in price from $250,000.

Saddest of all, the Cotton Mill, the heartbeat of the community, sat empty and neglected for a long time and was finally destroyed by fire. The only evidence that it ever existed is the office tower that still stands as well as the crumbling brick walls of the carpenter shop. The City of Atlanta made a nice park at the site to be enjoyed by a new generation of residents, people who have come in and bought and remodeled most of the old houses. As they say, "That's progress for you."

We know that in life nothing stays the same. The boys who were my age are now in their seventies, and the ones still standing meet the first Tuesday of each month for a fellowship breakfast to reminisce about those bygone days of playing coke stopper baseball, marble games such as "Granny" Knucks Down, playing For Keeps in the big ring, Mumbly Peg, Kack, and "Buckety Buck" and our many other made-up games. Gone are our various rituals, such as when you came out of the store with a Coke or RC Cola and Moon Pie you had to holler "none-ence" before someone else hollered "some-ance" which would mean you had to share with them. If you passed gas in a crowd you had to holler "bulger" before someone hollered "four pokes" and they would get to hit you on your arm four times. Strangest of all the rituals, when a new kid moved in or one was visiting a relative, they were held down and given a "pink belly."

Hopefully we have become a little more lenient by now, because at our age someone at our gathering would be hollering "bulger" every few minutes, and could not take the four hits.

"Those were the days."

Now city park, where mill existed.

Old carpenter shop.

163

The old company store, now apartments.

The ark (our first residence).

Ceremonial plaque dedicated to The Chattahoochee Boys at the old store.

Artist rendition of the old Whittier House. Artist: Shirley Newton Glosson

THE "CHATTAHOOCHEE BOYS"

Probably on a per capita basis we had more guys with nick-names than any other town in Georgia. There were some girls with nicknames, but they can't be repeated here.

Nicknames I remember, and there were probably more:

OLDER GENERATION:

Nose	Blob	Dude
Strawberry	Noe	Roosterman
Dink	Sonny Boy	Stinky
Buckshot	Bug	Boogerman
Blackie	Big 'Un	Runt
Soupbone	Red	Junior (2)
Cabbage	Thursday	Beedy
Shorty	Lightning	Snapper

MY GENERATION:

Pull	Sister	Nunu
Bootsie	Lefty	Turk
Titoe	Foots	Bug
Big Eye	Peewee	Barefoot
Two Weeks	Coal Box	Sonny
Flunkus	Sulkey Jane	Argie
Gussie	Welt	Junior (2)
Scrap Iron	Hatchet Head	Lucy
Slug	B.D.	Cotton

A number of these guys have "passed on," but I am sure that if there is a "company store" in God's Heaven, they are sitting on the store steps drinking an RC Cola and eating a Moon Pie, waiting for the rest of us to walk up and yell "Someance."

I took my son, Joe, on a journey today,
Back to the place where as a boy I would play.
The golf course is gone, all barren and red,
The dirt has been taken for bricks, instead.

The lakes that I fished in on many a day
Are now filled with trash there to rot and decay.
The round pond we swam in I no longer could find.
I wonder, did it exist only in my mind?

The ball field where many a thrill one recalls
Evicted the kids for old houses with halls.
Another place missing made my heart grow sadder,
It was fondly referred to as Grandpa's Ladder.

The only thing now seen by the eye undiluted
Is the old Chattahoochee now shamefully polluted.
Thank God for the memory of these places destroyed.
If only they'd been left for Joe to have enjoyed.

- June, 1969

Thanks to my wife, Martha, for the tedious task
of deciphering my handwritten notes and
putting it in a readable format.

Made in the USA
Columbia, SC
01 March 2020